Cambridge Elements ≡

Elements in Psychology and Culture
edited by
Kenneth D. Keith
University of San Diego

INDIGENOUS PSYCHOLOGY IN AFRICA

A Survey of Concepts, Theory, Research, and Praxis

Seth Oppong
University of Botswana

CAMBRIDGE
UNIVERSITY PRESS

Shaftesbury Road, Cambridge CB2 8EA, United Kingdom

One Liberty Plaza, 20th Floor, New York, NY 10006, USA

477 Williamstown Road, Port Melbourne, VIC 3207, Australia

314–321, 3rd Floor, Plot 3, Splendor Forum, Jasola District Centre, New Delhi – 110025, India

103 Penang Road, #05–06/07, Visioncrest Commercial, Singapore 238467

Cambridge University Press is part of Cambridge University Press & Assessment, a department of the University of Cambridge.

We share the University's mission to contribute to society through the pursuit of education, learning and research at the highest international levels of excellence.

www.cambridge.org
Information on this title: www.cambridge.org/9781009486972

DOI: 10.1017/9781009392860

First published 2024

A catalogue record for this publication is available from the British Library.

ISBN 978-1-009-48697-2 Hardback
ISBN 978-1-009-39284-6 Paperback
ISSN 2515-3986 (online)
ISSN 2515-3943 (print)

Indigenous Psychology in Africa

A Survey of Concepts, Theory, Research, and Praxis

Elements in Psychology and Culture

DOI: 10.1017/9781009392860
First published online: April 2024

Seth Oppong
University of Botswana

Abstract: Understanding human behaviour, thoughts, and emotional expressions can be challenging in the global context. Due to cultural differences, the study of psychology cannot be decontextualised. This calls for an unearthing of the explanatory systems that exist in Africa for understanding and accounting for the behaviour, emotions, and cognition of Africans. This call is addressed through the emergence of African psychology (AP) or Indigenous psychology in Africa (IPA) as a legitimate science of human experience. This Element discusses the motivations for AP, centrality of culture, demarcations of AP, and the different strands within AP. It highlights issues related to African philosophy, African cultural anthropology, African philosophy of science, and suitable methodological approaches for AP research. It also discusses some selected theoretical contributions and applications of AP. The Element concludes that AP researchers and practitioners need to pursue interdisciplinarity and avoid meaningless rejection of good ideas from other cultural settings.

Keywords: African psychology, indigenous psychology, African philosophy of science, African philosophy, applied African psychology

ISBNs: 9781009486972 (HB), 9781009392846 (PB), 9781009392860 (OC)
ISSNs: 2515-3986 (online), 2515-3943 (print)

Contents

A Note from the Series Editor

We were shocked and saddened to learn of the death of Seth Oppong on February 17, 2024. In his brief 41-year lifetime, Seth became a prolific author and researcher, and was a champion of Indigenous African psychology. Respected, admired, and loved by colleagues and students alike, he made his mark, not only in Africa, but internationally, as well. Seth was known for his kindness and wisdom, and an inspiration to those whom he encouraged and supported. We are fortunate to have this last work in the Elements series, and to see that he touches the lives of others one more time. We hope we have done justice to it in the final editing as it comes to print.

Kenneth D. Keith, April, 2024

1 Conceptual Foundations

1.1 Definitions

A good place to start an Element on Indigenous psychology in Africa (IPA) is to consider which terms are used synonymously with IPA. I have been criticised for using Indigenous psychology in Africa (IPA) rather than African psychology (AP). For instance, Augustine Nwoye takes issue with the use of 'IP' on the basis that it turns the limelight on the study of IP instead of AP in the current scholarship in psychology (Augustine Nwoye, personal communication, 7 July 2023). For Nwoye, the use of IP inadvertently gives the impression that AP is all about the study of culture and not actually psychology qua psychology; he argues that AP is concerned with not only the psychology of the pre-colonial Africans (African Indigenous psychology) but also the psychology and perturbations of contemporary or postcolonial Africans (Augustine Nwoye, personal communication, 7 July 2023). As much as I agree with Augustine Nwoye's concerns about the use of IP, the terminology I have used is 'IP in Africa'. Therefore, we shall use the acronym 'IPA' instead of 'IP' in Africa. This is to say that as much as Western psychology is a form of IP, IPA refers to a distinct body of psychological knowledge about and for Africa that contributes to global psychology in expanding the understanding of the human nature of all *Homo sapiens* (Oppong, 2022a). In this regard, IPA is used interchangeably with 'African psychology' (AP) and 'pan-African psychology' (PAP) (Oppong, 2022a). But what is AP really? Table 1 lists some of the definitions in use that can be applied to what we can call AP.

These definitions seem to share certain characteristics. All the definitions somewhat agree that AP or IPA (1) is an approach to doing psychological science in Africa, (2) emphasises the role of African culture, and (3) concerns theorising and empirical research in psychology. Thus, they all appear to say

Table 1 Selected definitions for African psychology/Indigenous psychology in Africa

Term	Definition	Source
Indigenous psychology, general	'an approach to research in psychology which stresses the importance of research being grounded in the conditions of the researcher's own society and culture' (p. 1)	Allwood (2018)
African psychology	'the systematic and informed study of the complexities of human mental life, culture and experience in the pre- and postcolonial African world' (p. 57)	Nwoye (2014)
Pan-African psychology	'a branch of psychology where the population of interest is persons of African origin, and/or where the target population resides either on the continent of Africa or in the Diaspora' (p. 10)	Oppong (2016)
African psychology	'ways of situating oneself in the field of psychology in relation to and from Africa' (p. 274)	Ratele (2017a)
IPA	'an orientation that adopts a culture-conscious approach to the selection of research questions, design, data analysis, and interpretation of results' (p. 956)	Oppong (2022a)

that AP must be embedded in the culture of the researchers to build up meaningful and locally relevant explanations for the behaviour, emotions, and cognition that underlie applications to the people in that locality. This also means that AP suggests research ought to begin from the culture rather than using lenses borrowed from outside the culture. Though Allwood is a non-African psychologist, his definition of IP serves a useful pedagogical purpose in outlining what IP generally is. This is consistent with Oppong's (2016) view that AP should not reject everything Western by virtue of just being Western but must critically review and use what may be considered useful.

A key question about IPA is who constitutes the people about whom and for whose benefit this psychological knowledge is being developed. Using Mazrui's (2005) classificatory scheme of Africans of the soil (including North Africans) and Africans by blood (including African Americans), Oppong (2016) identified four target groups for IP in Africa. They are (1) Africans by blood and of the soil (e.g., Ghana, Botswana, Cameroon, Nigeria, Kenya, Uganda, etc.); (2) Africans by blood but not of the soil (Black Americans, Afro-Caribbeans, etc.); (3) Africans not by blood but of the soil (mostly the non-Black inhabitants of North Africa and various non-Black populations in different parts of the continent of Africa); and (4) Africans not by blood and not of the soil (naturalised citizens of various African countries). Towards this end, Oppong (2016, p. 10) argues that IPA is an indigenous psychology in which both Africans of the soil and by blood are the

> target population due to their shared history, conditions of living, values, and traditions. These shared attributes include slavery, colonialism, neocolonialism, coloniality, racism, poverty, diseases, damaged self-identity, spirituality, art, communalism, respect for elderly, nature-human harmony, and a host of others.

Another important question to raise and respond to is: is IPA the study of the psychology of Indigenous peoples in Africa? The United Nations (UN, 2004, p. 2) defines Indigenous peoples as peoples and nations that:

> hav[e] a historical continuity with pre-invasion and pre-colonial societies that developed on their territories, consider themselves distinct from other sectors of the societies now prevailing on those territories, or parts of them. They form at present non-dominant sectors of society and are determined to preserve, develop and transmit to future generations their ancestral territories, and their ethnic identity, as the basis of their continued existence as peoples, in accordance with their own cultural patterns, social institutions and legal system.

There have been some debates as to whether the term 'Indigenous' has the same meaning in Africa as elsewhere. The key argument is that 'all Africans are indigenous to Africa in the sense that they were there before the European colonialists arrived and that they have been subject to sub-ordination during colonialism' (African Commission on Human and Peoples' Rights [ACHPR] & International Work Group for Indigenous Affairs [IWGIA], 2005, p. 88). Thus, it assumed that it is not proper to ascribe 'Indigenous' status to a few communities. However, ACHPR and IWGIA (2005, p. 89) argued that recognition of Indigenous peoples in Africa ought to be based on whether the culture and lifeways of the groups that identify as Indigenous peoples can be differentiated significantly from 'the dominant society and their cultures[, which] are under threat in some cases to the point of extinction'. Therefore, it must be understood that Africa's stance on Indigenous peoples differs from other parts of the world. As a result, ACHPR and IWGIA (2005) recognised certain groups as Indigenous communities (see Table 2).

Nonetheless, IPA should not be assumed to be about only those who identify as or were identified by ACHPR and IWGIA (2005) as Indigenous peoples but rather as targeting every African as the object of its study. This is because, by the very definition from the UN (2004), all Africans are Indigenous. However, the use of the term Indigenous peoples should be reserved for those identified in Table 2 to draw attention to their marginalisation in contemporary Africa. Therefore, the use of the term IPA must be understood to communicate that one is studying, more or less, a truly authentic psychology of Africans that has not been adulterated by Western influence. However, it is not, or should not be considered, a form of romanticising the African 'glorious' past. Instead, IPA is about the contemporary life lived and experienced by Africans with meanings derived from the past to guide both current and future behaviours, thoughts, and

Table 2 Examples of Indigenous peoples/communities in Africa

Category	Community/People
Hunter-gatherers	Pygmies of the Great Lakes Region, the San of Southern Africa, the Hadzabe of Tanzania, and the Ogiek of Kenya.
Pastoralists and agro-pastoralist	The Pokot of Kenya and Uganda, the Barabaig of Tanzania, the Maasai of Kenya and Tanzania, the Samburu, Turkana, Rendille, Orma, and Borana of Kenya and Ethiopia, the Karamojong of Uganda, the isolated pastoralist communities in Sudan, Somalia, and Ethiopia, the Touareg and Fulani of Mali, Burkina-Faso, and Niger, and the Mbororo in Cameroon and other West African countries.

Source: ACHPR and IWGIA (2005, pp. 15–19); African Development Bank Group (2016, pp. 10–11)

emotional expressions (see Nwoye, 2015a; Oppong, 2022a; Weber et al., 2021). More forcefully, Mpofu (2002, p. 182) reminds us that the critics of cross-cultural studies and applications of theories (in this case, critics of Western hegemonic psychology in Africa) do not have to 'have a romantic view of their own or other cultures as cut in stone or unchanging'. This is because such criticism has 'the limitation of failing to take regard of how cultures evolve under their own impetus and in interaction with other cultures' (Mpofu, 2002, p. 182). He further argues that even 'if psychological theories unique to African settings were developed, they would still not be wholly applicable to all African societies and would have to contend with much the same criticisms as currently leveled against those developed in Western societies' (Mpofu, 2002, p. 182). This is a good reminder that 'Africa is not a museum', to borrow from Weber et al. (2021, p. 1), and that culture is dynamic.

I share similar sentiments about the unfortunate romanticism of African pasts. This is a view that particularly applies in cases where Western scholars interested in the psychology of Africans and African culture tend to have a romantic view of African culture and attempt to revive a long-forgotten past. For instance, Allwood (2018) was fascinated by our advocacy for the eradication of what we called outmoded cultural practices (Oppong, Asante, & Oppong, 2012). I wish here to reiterate the caution given by Mpofu (2002) that African culture is not static while 'Africa is not a museum' (Weber et al., 2021, p. 1). That we advocate for an AP does not mean we are not alive to the fact that every culture has a set of harmful and progressive practices, to which Africa is no exception. Thus, we call for the eradication of harmful cultural practices in order to promote the well-being of the African in the modern world. Therefore, there is nothing wrong with borrowing useful ideas from other cultures (see Ahuma, 1905) as long as it promotes community and individual well-being. However, the process of eradication should be done in a respectful manner so that the community does not vehemently resist the transformation. It may also be useful to take a functional perspective – borrowing from sociology – that considers the functions of each harmful cultural practice and works with and through the community to formulate a harmless substitution or replacement that prevents disorientation among community members. This is often lacking in attempts to eradicate harmful cultural practices in African communities by Western outsiders.

1.2 Centrality of Culture

The relationship between culture and behaviour is well documented (Sam, 2014). The question of culture leads one to wonder if there is anything like an African culture. Does Africa have a monolithic culture? I do not think that there is a monolithic African culture per se. Culture should also not be used in a vague manner to mean any material differences between or among people. Spencer-Oatey (2008) considered culture a shared set of assumptions and orientations to life that has the potential to influence behaviour and its meanings among a collective. Further, Kluckhohn and Kelly (1945) defined culture as the 'designs for living ... which exist at any given time as potential guides for ... [human] behaviour' (p. 97). It is due to the use of mere material differences as an expression of culture that led Poortinga (2021) to argue for dispensing with the term 'culture' in (cross-)cultural psychology for its vagueness when used psychologically. Thus, Poortinga (2021) believes that culture ought to be 'defined in terms of specific variables or behavior domains rather than in terms of some poorly defined part of the behavior repertoire' (p. 25).

In questioning the idea of a monolithic African culture, Allwood (2018, 2019) asked if: (1) there are common traits across the African continent, and (2) it is scientifically feasible to identify such continental traits. There are only about three ways to resolve this problem. First, we can consider personal experiences of an African traversing the continent. When an African traverses the continent, one cannot help but see the similarities underneath the *visible* differences that you would find in behaviours, belief systems, emotional expressions, and cognitions. In this sense, one can argue that, although there are *visible* differences in behavioural patterns, they appear to converge around common themes that make one African not very different from another. The *visible* differences are possibly due to differences in the physical environment given that culture represents a guide for living. Thus, if you find yourself in a forest area where the soil is viable for tubers (cassava, yam, etc.), you will evolve a tuber-based food habit. If you find yourself in an area where the soil is suitable for growing cotton, you will produce cotton-based fabrics for your use. Though these differences (food habits and style of clothing) are part of culture, they are often the direct responses to the physical environmental conditions, and they do not represent shared assumptions and orientations to life. These responses to the physical environment may also show up in the understanding of the fundamental relationship between humans and between humans and the environment. However, these assumptions about human–environment relations should not be taken to mean they are at the core of culture. Rather, they act as constraints on how one can make sense of one's world. They are important but they may not be the essence of the culture.

Second, we can also view the question of a monolithic African culture through a theoretical framework. One of the useful theories of culture that serves this purpose is Schein's (1984, 2004) levels-of-culture theory. This theory is useful because it helps to analyse culture at different levels. Within this theory, there are three levels of analysis of culture, namely, (1) observable artefacts and behaviours, (2) espoused values and beliefs, and (3) underlying assumptions (Oppong & Strader, 2022; Schein, 1984, 2004). When one traverses the continent of Africa, one notes there are observable differences in terms of clothes, language, food, arts, parenting styles, and a host of other things that we can see, hear, and feel (Oppong & Strader, 2022). Needless to say, these observable patterns reflect the most *visible* level of cultural artefacts. However, most people end their analysis at this level and presume that these African cultures are indeed different. A deeper analysis of African cultures at the *invisible* (below-the-surface) levels of espoused values and beliefs and underlying assumptions tends to reveal some commonalities across the continent. These are commonalities in values and assumptions with which keen observers are often confronted. Behaviour might differ from one African community to another but the purpose it serves may essentially be the same. Though it is advisable not to think of a monolithic African culture, there are some commonalities at deeper levels of analysis beyond what is visible or observable. Consistent with this perspective, Mkhize (2013, pp. 34–5) argues that

> African scholars are not in agreement about the existence of unifying African worldview or metaphysics . . . Although there may not be a unifying African metaphysics, there is nevertheless *an approach to reality* [emphasis added] shared by a number of Africans. Its central tenets about beliefs about God, the universe and notions of causality, person and time.
>
> Thus, there is an African approach to reality that appears different from other cultures.

Last, we can also answer this question based on emerging theorising and empirical work from Africa-based scholars. At the level of theorising, Gyekye's (2003) philosophical work is relevant here. He drew on maxims from diverse African traditions to construct a set of African cultural values. Specifically, Gyekye (2003) drew on maxims from ethnic groups across Africa such as the Akan (Ghana, West Africa), Ewe (Ghana, West Africa), Yoruba (Nigeria, West Africa), Igbos (Nigeria, West Africa), Benin (Nigeria, West Africa), Basotho (Lesotho, Southern Africa), Ndebele (Zimbabwe, Southern Africa), and Swahili (Kenya, Tanzania, Democratic Republic of the Congo, Uganda, Burundi, Rwanda, and Mozambique; East Africa). Together, the languages spoken by these ethnic groups cut across four language families identified by linguistics as those most widely spoken in various parts of the continent: Niger-Congo, Nilo-Saharan, Afro-Asiatic, and Indo-European. This is very important to note because language is a reflection of one's worldview (see Sapir-Whorf hypothesis; Whorf, 1956). Thus, language is a sort of institutional memory of a group of people, though it is always evolving. Given the various language families represented in Gyekye's (2003) philosophical exploration, we can confidently say that he covered most of Africa to produce African cultural values, which he outlined as, namely, (1) religious values, (2) values of humanity and brotherhood, (3) communal and individualistic values, (4) moral values, (5) family values, (6) economic values including African conceptions of work ethic, (7) chieftaincy and political values, (8) aesthetic values, (9) values for knowledge and wisdom, (10) human rights values, and (11) values for ancestorship and tradition. Together, these values help to understand the African approach to reality. And these values are, more or less, the same as those detected by the keen observer despite the visible differences in behavioural patterns. It is like saying: we are the same at heart.

Furthermore, Oppong (2020b) employed ethnographic studies on cognitive abilities in Africa to formulate an African conception of cognitive abilities, the so-named model of valued human cognitive abilities. I employed ethnographic studies done in Zambia (Southern Africa), Kenya (East Africa), and Togo (West Africa). Like Gyekye (2003), I employed the same four language families (Niger-Congo, Nilo-Saharan, Afro-Asiatic, and Indo-European) with the advantages of wider coverage in this systematic review. This work does not directly relate to cultural values per se, but the evidence can be taken to mean that it is possible to identify commonalities across the continent of Africa. Again, if we take values to mean that which is important for a group of people and guides their actions, then the formulation of the African conceptions of cognitive abilities may also be seen as those aspects of cognitive abilities important to Africans and that guide their actions towards developing those abilities in themselves and the next generation of Africans. Taken together, these projects suggest that there may be an African approach to reality. So, to answer the question of whether or not there is a monolithic African culture, it is a 'no', but there seems to be an African approach to reality that underlies the diverse ways of behaving, thinking, and feeling across the continent.

On a final note, we need to address the question of the status of African Indigenous peoples' culture in AP. As argued earlier, ACHPR and IWGIA (2005, p. 89) advocate for the recognition of Indigenous peoples based on whether the culture and lifeways of the groups that identify as Indigenous peoples can be differentiated significantly from 'the dominant society and their cultures[, which] are under threat in some cases to the point of extinction' (see 1.1 Definitions). As a result, there is a danger that African Indigenous peoples' culture would be further marginalised, resulting in double marginalisation. For instance, the San People of Botswana view their culture as under threat and are concerned about the limited integration of their cultural values and language into the mainstream educational system of Botswana (Ketsitlile, 2013; Mafela, 2014; Molosiwa & Galeforolwe, 2018). This is true of other Indigenous peoples in Africa, including the Maasai of Kenya and Tanzania; the Hadzabe of Tanzania; the Ogiek of Kenya; the Touareg and Fulani of Mali, Burkina-Faso, and Niger, to mention a few. Thus, it is more likely that AP scholars may, knowingly or unknowingly, perpetuate the further marginalisation of African Indigenous peoples and their culture. In other words, there is and may continue to be colonisation of marginalised Africans by other formerly colonised Africans whose culture is now mainstream in contemporary Africa – a situation that should be prevented or avoided by any means. Therefore, it is vital that AP scholars explore and integrate African Indigenous peoples' culture into mainstream AP. Indeed, there must be special topics on African Indigenous peoples' culture in any study of AP. Again, the decolonial gaze should also be turned on the colonising African of mainstream society to make them understand that they are perpetuating the very institution they abhor against fellow Africans.

1.3 Demarcating IPA

Is IPA a subfield or an orientation or a movement? To be able to sufficiently answer this question, one will need to consider what makes a domain a subfield in psychology. Currently, there are no clear guidelines in psychology as to when an area of research is established enough to become a subfield. As a result, I will employ literature on the sociology of professions. Thus, the question to ask is: what makes a domain a profession? Greenwood (1976) outlined the possession of a core body of knowledge (theory), authority from that expertise, community sanction or acceptance of that authority, ethical codes, and culture as the key characteristics of a profession. If we take these characteristics as embodiments of a subfield, one will reach a conclusion that IPA is not a subfield, nor does it have what it takes at this moment to be a subfield within psychology at any time soon. This is because, as a domain, it does not currently have a core canon theory, community sanction or legitimacy even among all Africa-based psychologists, and culture of its own (I use the term 'African psychologists' to refer to Africa-based psychologists who truly pursue AP or IPA; the former is defined by an approach and the latter by geography). Thus, it is difficult to conceive of IPA as a subfield or foresee the possibility of it becoming a subfield.

Similarly, Hambrick and Chen (2008) have argued that academic fields usually begin as informal communities of academics who view their agenda in the discipline as permanent in some way and believe that they cannot achieve their agenda by continuing to exist as an informal community. Thus, these

informal communities push for independence and eventually, when their arguments are widely known and accepted, they become subfields. When there is an
informal community of academics, we can agree that a movement is being
formed within the discipline. When judged against these conditions, one will
also realise that IPA is nowhere near the possibility of constituting itself into an
academic field nor is it a movement with a following in the discipline of
psychology. For instance, there is no informal community of scholars with
a psychological sense of community to establish IPA as an academic field.
This is because there never has been a grouping of Africa-based psychologists
who identify as key participants in IPA or use a label that purports to describe
them as such. There have never been any periodic meetings of Africa-based
psychologists interested in IPA, nor do they represent most Africa-based psychologists (Nwoye, 2014; Oppong, 2022a; Ratele, 2017a, 2017c). However, there
was a one-day workshop on Empirical Directions for a Decolonial Psychology
held on Monday, 22 May 2023, at Stellenbosch University, South Africa, that
invited some Africa-based psychologists, including me. This meeting was,
however, not necessarily an attempt to create a psychological sense of community but rather discussed ways to analyse data from an IPA orientation. It would
be safe to say that most of the Africa-based psychologists interested in IPA are
based in South Africa, though there are pockets of others across the continent of
Africa. It is somewhat understandable as to why there are fewer Africa-based
psychologists who identify with Africanisation of psychology. This is because
many Africans exist in monoracial spaces and 'are less likely to recognise the
existence of inequalities in knowledge production, let alone attribute such
inequalities to race' (Oppong, 2022a, p. 955). Given that South Africa is
a multiracial space, they 'easily comprehend the Euro-American hegemony,
coloniality, and the pursuit of decolonialism' (Oppong, 2022a, p. 955). This is
not to suggest that South Africa is the only multiracial space in Africa; there are
others like Namibia, Zimbabwe, Kenya, Tunisia, and other parts of North Africa
with pockets in Angola, Zambia, Mozambique, Tanzania, Congo, Senegal, and
Gabon. Here, multiracial space implies a collective of racially diverse members
with unevenly distributed power who exist and interact over a period with the
uneasy option of non-participation (Oppong, 2022a). The space may be
a country, state, university, or any community of people. This does not mean
that there shall ever be an equal distribution of power in any group, but when
people of diverse races exist in the same space, there shall always be the race
with more power and the other with less power.

What about IPA as an orientation? Among other things, Merriam-Webster
(n.d.) defines 'orientation' as a general or lasting direction of thought,
inclination, or interest. This definition implies that an orientation is identifiable

whenever there is a set of attitudes, beliefs, or inclinations with respect to a particular subject or issue. This can be at the level of an individual or a group. Indigenous psychology in Africa tends to represent an approach by a few Africa-based psychologists. These Africa-based psychologists tend to share a certain belief that the Euro-American-centric body of knowledge in psychology is inadequate and, sometimes, misleading in its capacity to account for the experiences of Africans. This view seems to represent an orientation more than a subfield or a movement. This implies that IPA is more likely to be an orientation. But does an orientation have the capacity to evolve into a movement and later a subfield? A very reasonable way of answering this question is to revisit how academic fields are formed. The existence of an informal community of academics may also imply that the members of that community tend to share a common orientation in their field broadly and consider their continued existence on the fringes of the discipline would not serve their agenda well. Thus, one can argue that sharing an orientation may be a precondition for the academic research domain to become an established subfield. In this sense, it is possible to say that IPA has the chance of evolving into an academic field in its own right. However, the fact that most Africans exist in monoracial spaces will delay or even hinder the evolution of the orientation into a movement. In this regard, I dare say that IPA, though an orientation, has a long way to go to become a movement and finally an academic subfield.

1.4 Strands of IPA

If we agree that IPA exists as an orientation in its current form, we can then explore the question of whether there is only a single strand. In his classificatory scheme, Ratele (2017a, 2017c) identifies four strands of orientations within IPA or AP, namely: (1) Western-oriented AP; (2) psychological African studies; (3) cultural AP; and (4) critical AP. A Western-oriented AP is simply the study of behaviour in African settings using Western theories, methods, and tools with the assumption that psychology can be a universal, decontextualised science characterised by apolitical stance and objectivity (Ratele, 2017a, 2017c). Identifying with this strand of IPA requires less work; one simply imitates and conducts research to close the gaps in 'global' psychological literature. The Western-oriented AP tends to have a large following in Africa. Despite this, it is not to be confused with an orientation in IPA. This orientation produces knowledge that is consistent with the mainstream ideas in Western psychology. Therefore, it is safe to say that psychological African studies, cultural AP, and critical AP are the three main orientations in IPA.

Cultural AP appears to be the psychological study of African people as embedded in metaphysical, spiritual, or cultural contexts (Ratele, 2017a, 2017c). Africa-based psychologists who identify with cultural AP tend to be concerned with the psychological exploration of African peoples as reflected in 'African language, values, beliefs, worldviews, philosophies, and knowledge' (Ratele, 2017c, p. 320). Similarly, critical AP refers to the study of the inter-penetration between power and knowledge with respect to the continent and Africans broadly and more specifically in psychology (Ratele, 2017a, 2017c). Researchers who identify with critical AP tend to preoccupy themselves with issues that relate to 'power, privilege, oppression, and alienation, in their various manifestations (such as political, economic, intellectual, gender, pro-fessional, as well as cultural power)' (Ratele, 2017c, p. 322). Indeed, this strand of IPA tends to focus on colonialism and the resultant need to decolonise hegemonic psychology. Finally, psychological African studies is concerned with psychologically or psychoanalytically inclined African studies aimed at 'integrating the theories, tools, and insights of the field into studies of Africa' (Ratele, 2017c, p. 323). Therefore, psychological African studies tends to uphold interdisciplinarity and transdisciplinarity in that it embraces literature from disciplines such as history, politics, economics, anthropology, philosophy, languages and literature, and religion if their focus is on Africa and Africans. While the classificatory scheme is important to enable us to engage in concep-tual discussions, in practice, there may not be any Africa-based psychologist who fits neatly into a particular strand. Thus, you are more likely to find Africa-based psychologists whose work traverses the four strands. One can identify certain individuals whose research may be, more or less, in a particular strand (see Table 3).

However, upon closer inspection, one can find most of the different strands of IPA in a single work of the psychologists associated with a particular strand or who do different work using different strands of IPA. For instance, Augustine Bame Nsamenang's work on child development tends to have cultural and critical strands of IPA, while Ratele's work can be found in both psychological African studies and critical AP domains. In this respect, it would be safe to say that some Africa-based psychologists cannot fit neatly into any of the strands but tend to work from whichever strand or combinations of strands provide adequate tools to conduct their research. Thus, in addition to Ratele's (2017a, 2017c) classification, I will add an *AP-informed multiple perspectives* strand in IPA. This strand allows Africa-based psychologists to operate within one strand or several at a time but can traverse strands if need be.

A concern that can possibly be raised is why I did not include Western-oriented AP, identified by Ratele in Table 3. In response, I argue that Western-oriented AP

Table 3 Examples of African psychologists associated with the strands of IPA

Strand	Researcher
Cultural AP	Augustine Nwoye, Bame Nsamenang, Robert Serpell, Nhlanhla Mkhize, David Luckman Sam, Richard Appiah, Godfrey Ejuu (i.e., child research)
Critical AP	Derek Hook, Peace Kiguwa, Wahbie Long, Tamara Shefer
Psychological African studies	Kopano Ratele, Glenn Adams, Vivian Afi Dzokoto, Mamadou Diouf, Achille Mbembe, Annabella Osei-Tutu
AP-informed multiple perspectives	Seth Oppong, Steven Adjei Baffour

Note: African psychologists refer to Africa-based psychologists pursuing AP as opposed to those merely located in Africa who happen to be psychologists (Western-oriented Africa-based psychologists).

is not necessarily AP in a true sense. Work done in this strand provides points of critique just like work done in Western psychology. In this regard, I tend to agree with Nwoye that Western-oriented AP should not be considered AP as it constitutes Western psychology in Africa (Augustine Nwoye, personal communication, 7 July 2023). This is because Western-oriented AP continues to skew 'nearly all theoretical explanations, frames what is taught, influences what is published and the research approaches and analyses' towards Western epistemologies (Ratele, 2017c, p. 319). In addition, attempts to indigenise psychology in Africa are often greeted by researchers in so-called Western-oriented AP as efforts to devalue the scientific status of psychology (Naidoo, 1996). It is almost as if they are saying you cannot set your own standards and that Africa-based psychologists should be standard-followers (Oppong, 2019a; Ssentongo, 2020). In sum, cultural AP, critical AP, psychological African studies, and AP-informed multiple perspectives tend to reflect what we will consider main elements or strands of IPA or AP. Thus, in this Element, when I talk about IPA or AP, I am referring to these different elements and exclude the Western-oriented AP first identified by Ratele (2017a, 2017c). This, I believe, will represent a general consensus among Africa-based psychologists who work within the space of AP or IPA.

It is also worth noting that this scheme of classification of the different strands of IPA has been heavily criticised (Nwoye, 2017c). The central criticism is that such a scheme risks presenting IPA as 'a decentred field of study' being carried out in 'heterogeneous terrains' (Nwoye, 2017c, p. 332). To Nwoye (2017c), this implies that IPA is depicted not to 'aspire to the status of a full-fledged field of postcolonial studies located within the university discipline of Psychology but rather as an orientation or approach to the study of Psychology in the African context' (p. 332). Further, he argues that depicting IPA as an orientation to the study of psychology fails to equally endow Africa-based psychology with the capacity to develop IPA into a subfield.

In response, I argue that the classificatory system does not seem to me to suggest that IPA is a decentred field of study of psychology but rather that there are different orientations to doing IPA that have evolved in Africa. In many ways, this concern appears to be similar to the different schools of psychology that emerged at the beginning of Western psychology and eventually culminated into different subfields. I dare say, rather, that the early recognition of the different strands of IPA holds potential for Africa-based psychologists to develop them into initial subfields of IPA. As I have argued earlier (see 1.3 Demarcating IPA), IPA appears for now to be an orientation rather than a movement in Africa. Therefore, this IPA orientation will have to become a movement to gain momentum before it becomes a subfield. However, I am hopeful that IPA will eventually become a subfield with its own orientations – these orientations will more likely evolve from the strands of IPA discussed earlier.

1.5 Decolonisation Theme in IPA

Within Ratele's (2017c) classificatory system, critical AP is the only one that seems to be largely concerned with coloniality and decolonisation. This is because of the desire to interrogate the material concerns of the African and their manifestations. If we take it that several Africa-based psychologists in IPA tend to assume the multiple perspectives strand, then we can say that decolonisation is a central question within IPA. Decolonisation can be understood to imply efforts at dismantling 'the colonial institutional structures (with their associated power dynamics) that assign epistemic centre status to select groups or geographic regions or languages in a postcolonial world', while indigenisation means efforts that ensure we 'embrace the perspectives and methods of knowing inherent in a local culture as valid ontology and epistemology' (Oppong, 2022a, p. 955). More specifically, Pickren and Taşçı (2022) argue that 'Decolonization is aimed at states, institutions of the state, land, place, or what is instantiated or material' (p. 12). Therefore, 'To decolonize is to seek to replace or supplant the governance of those institutions [universities, journals, disciplines, societies, etc.] or at least gain recognition from them' (p. 12). The relationship between the decolonisation and indigenisation has been resolved such that indigenisation has been viewed as one of the approaches to decolonisation (see Pickren & Taşçı, 2022). This means that to decolonise will necessarily involve indigenising as well, though the opposite may not be true.

The central question of decolonisation is relevant to all the strands of IPA. This is because there is an imbalance of power with the current predominant Western-oriented AP placing most Africa-based psychologists at the bottom of the global hierarchy of knowledge production. In one breath, it is unfair, but on the other hand, it is broadly understandable. Lamont (2019, p. 34) argues that if one does not do 'original, daring, [and] stimulating' work, no one is likely to notice the work being done. Much of the work done in Western-oriented AP tends to be imitative (Ratele, 2017a, 2017c). More generally, work done by African social scientists is mocked for being heavily data-driven and less conceptual and theoretical (Yankah, 2012). What this means is that Western-oriented AP is less likely to make significant contributions in the discipline of psychology because of its imitative nature. Thus, decolonising psychology helps to create space for intellectually diverse understandings of human behaviour to co-exist with the mainstream perspectives. This then makes it possible for gatekeepers in knowledge dissemination (in psychology) to be open to the need for different perspectives on human behaviour, emotions, and cognition to be disseminated. This is how the global community of psychologists becomes welcoming of works cast in the strands of IPA (see Table 2). In other words, cultural AP, critical AP, psychological African studies, and multiple perspectives AP will fail to take root or be taken seriously if psychology itself is not first decolonised. This idea of decolonisation of psychology as a prerequisite for the strands of IPA to flourish is why decolonisation finds its way into the different strands of IPA, even though it is closely related to critical AP. Thus, there cannot be an IPA without decolonisation.

Perhaps it is important to note here that, to some scholars, the power of Indigenous psychologies is that they are by the people for the people, and regardless of what Western psychology is doing, it has inherent worth and value. Though this position is true to some degree, Yang's (2012) classificatory system of different psychologies is very useful in the context of the argument about decolonisation. Yang (2012) distinguishes among folk, philosophical, and scientific psychologies. He regards folk psychology as 'the ordinary psychological views, assumptions, beliefs, concepts, conjectures, theories, preferences, norms, and practices that have been naturally and gradually acquired through socialization and that are commonly held by the general population of a society' (Yang, 2012, p. 3). He also considers philosophical psychology as 'the formal systems of psychological thought as proposed by a society's philosophers' (Yang, 2012, p. 3). Further, he defines scientific psychology as 'a psychological knowledge system constructed by academic or expert psychologists using scientific methodology' (Yang, 2012, p. 3). Though Indigenous psychology has inherent worth and value, it is more of the folk psychology. Thus, decolonisation breaks barriers to the inclusion of folk and philosophical psychologies in the scientific psychology by the academics and scholars of the Majority World.

1.6 Significance of Establishing IPA

Why is IPA important and for whom? At the outset, I would say an IPA is good for 'global' psychology. IPA responds to different needs. First, it responds to the issue of poor fit between the theories of hegemonic psychology and the lived realities of Africans. This has been the major call for indigenising the discipline of psychology in Africa (Nwoye, 2015a; Oppong, 2016, 2022a; Ratele, 2017a, 2017b, 2017c). There is a recognition that the explanatory framework of hegemonic psychology fails to explain so many aspects of the life of the African that there is a need to develop or expand existing explanatory frameworks (see Jahoda, 2016). For instance, Nwoye (2015a) outlines a number of differences between Western and African psychologies, including the emphasis on (1) the use of quantification in Western psychology while IPA emphasises holistic approaches to the study of human nature; (2) the material essence of humans in Western psychology whereas IPA emphasises human religiosity and spirituality; (3) the observable without the need for interpretation in Western psychology while IPA emphasises symbolism with meaning beyond the observed; and (4) the ancestorship and the land of the dead in IPA whereas Western psychology accepts as given that the mind ceases to exist upon the physical death of the body. Indeed, the differences identified by Nwoye (2015a) seem to be a summarised version of those African cultural values identified by Gyekye (2003). For emphasis, I repeat Gyekye's (2003) African cultural values here: (1) religious values, (2) values of humanity and brotherhood, (3) communal and individualistic values, (4) moral values, (5) family values, (6) economic values including African conceptions of work ethic, (7) chieftaincy and political values, (8) aesthetic values, (9) values for knowledge and wisdom, (10) human rights values, and (11) values for ancestorship and tradition. These differences can produce different understandings of human nature. For instance, most Africans believe the mind is penetrable (Dzokoto, 2020) to the extent that there is a strong belief that mental health challenges can be attributed to spiritual causes (Asare & Danquah, 2017; Mbiti, 1969; Nwoye, 2015a, 2015b; Opare-Henaku & Utsey, 2017; Oppong, 2020a). Thus, Oppong (2020a, p. 469) has suggested that mental health professionals ought to 'acknowledge this belief without devaluing it while using this belief to encourage adherence to treatment'. This approach to spirituality will seem very different from providing therapy to members of Western societies. However, it should not be assumed that there are no religious persons from Western societies. It is just that 'African peoples do not know how to exist without religion' (Mbiti, 1969, p. 2), implying that there is no life without religion in Africa or that religion serves as the life force for daily functioning of the African. This is linked to the observation that Africans tend to operate within an interpreted universe (Nwoye, 2015a).

In addition, Africa has been under-represented in the psychological body of knowledge (Arnett, 2008; Draper et al., 2022; Rad et al., 2018; Scheidecker, Chaudhary et al., 2023; Singh et al., 2023; Thalmayer et al., 2021). The hegemonic psychological body of knowledge serves as the foundation for theorising about human behaviour across the world. However, this under-representation of African research participants in published psychology literature limits the generalizability of the evidence (see Oppong, 2020b, 2019a, 2015a). Thus, any attempt to comprehensively create and advocate for the creation of IPA serves to expand global psychology to a truly global science of all humans.

Another motivation for indigenising psychology is that psychology in Africa is dominated by Western-oriented AP; this state of affairs reflects a less desirable situation where psychology in Africa is a mere mimicry of Western psychology. Indeed, this Western-oriented AP skews 'nearly all theoretical explanations, frames what is taught, influences what is published and the research approaches and analyses' towards Western epistemologies (Ratele, 2017c, p. 319). It is worth noting that many Africa-based psychologists recognise the challenge in applying Western psychology to many Africans, particularly those in the informal sector of the economy and those in rural settings in Africa; there appears to be a lack of inertia, preventing change. Naidoo (1996) explains that this inertia may be due to fears that challenging the core assumptions of Western-oriented AP may devalue the scientific status of the psychology with which they pride themselves. Perhaps another useful insight relates to the quest by Africa-based psychologists to be considered and viewed by Western knowledge gatekeepers and psychologists as 'good boys' or 'good girls' to be published, which serves to reinforce this inertia (Oppong, 2019a; Yankah, 2012).

2 African Philosophy as an Essential Foundation of AP

In this section, I will attempt to highlight the fact that Western psychology is derived partly from Western philosophy and that any attempt to develop IPA should also be informed by African philosophy. First, most psychologists would agree that Western psychology evolved out of Western philosophy and physiology (Hergenhahn, 2009; Oppong, 2017, 2022a; Oppong et al., 2023; Ratele 2017a, 2017c; Teo & Febbraro, 2003). In this regard, I have argued that psychology can be said to be the study of philosophy by other means (see Oppong 2017). I cite some examples here to illustrate the fact that hegemonic psychology (and psychological inquiry) derives from and is underpinned by Western philosophical thoughts and considerations, and, sometimes, produces forced consensuses. For instance, Francis Bacon (1561–1626), through the Baconian inductive method, influenced Burrhus Frederic Skinner's (1904–1990) operant conditioning. Bacon's atheoretical philosophy was adopted by Skinner, in which one tries out different ideas or conditions until they find one that works (Hergenhahn, 2009). Like Bacon, Skinner also believed that the primary purpose of science is to improve the human condition (Hergenhahn, 2009). This view of the purpose of science has been challenged recently to the effect that the primary purpose of science is theory, as good theories are what can improve human conditions (see Oppong, 2022b).

Though presentist to a degree, Rene Descartes's (1596–1650) mechanistic explanations of behaviour can be viewed as foundational to the emergence of the stimulus-response (S-R) theory and radical behaviourism in hegemonic psychology. In explaining reflexes, Descartes conceived of the sensory receptors in the sense organs as pressure plates that were linked to the brain by nerves; he thought that the nerves were hollow tubes that hold 'delicate threads" connecting sensory receptors to the cavities or ventricles in the brain (Hergenhahn, 2009; Schultz & Schultz, 2012). This philosophical thought allowed for an explanation of how sensory inputs from the environment impact the body without any intermediary. This became the essence of the S-R theory – once there is a stimulus, the organism will react in the expected direction of that stimulus.

David Hume's (1711–1776) exposition on the laws of association of ideas and analysis of causation influenced approaches to experimentation in psychology (Hergenhahn, 2009). For instance, Hume observed that in order to conclude that two events are causally related, the following conditions must hold: (1) the two events must occur in sequence in both space and time, (2) the presumed cause must occur before the presumed effect, (3) there must also be a relation between the two events, and (4) the presumed same cause should always lead to the presumed effect and the same presumed effect only occurs as result of the presumed cause (Flew, 1962; Hergenhahn, 2009). A century later, John Stuart Mill (1806–73) is reported to have also made a similar observation, that (1) the presumed cause should precede the presumed effect, (2) there must be a relation between the presumed cause and the presumed effect, and (3) there must not be any plausible alternative reason for the presumed effect other than the presumed cause (Shadish et al., 2002). Currently, this logic of causation has evolved into the following: (1) the *principle of temporal order*, that the presumed causal factor precedes the presumed effect, (2) the *principle of covariation*, that the presumed cause covaries with the effect such that changes in the cause correspond to changes in the effect, (3) the *principle of control*, that the alternative explanations have been ruled out, and (4) the *principle of counterfactual inference*, that there should be knowledge about what would have happened in the absence of the cause (see Shadish et al., 2002).

Others, like Johann Wolfgang von Goethe (1749–1832), Baruch Spinoza (1632– 77), and Friedrich Wilhelm Nietzsche (1844–1900), have also influenced Western psychology. For instance, Johann Wolfgang von Goethe provided the foundations for phenomenology in the social and behavioural sciences, while Baruch Spinoza's philosophical work on emotions served as the basis for work on emotions as a construct in psychology as well as psychoanalytic thinking (Hergenhahn, 2009). Again, Friedrich Wilhelm Nietzsche's notion of the Dionysian aspect of human nature as *das es* influenced the development of Sigmund Freud's (1856–1939) idea of *id* while Nietzsche's exposition on the concept of repression also became foundational to Freudian psychoanalysis (Hergenhahn, 2009). The foregoing discussion leaves no doubt in anybody's mind that Western philosophy is the foundation of today's Western psychology.

The taken-for-granted interpenetration between Western psychology and Western philosophy is further legitimised and strengthened by the recognition that all human sciences must necessarily confront a philosophical question, a response to which conditions the principles and methods of the discipline (Oppong et al., 2023). Like other human sciences, psychology takes as its subject of study the human being and behaviour of people. It is worthy of note that the quest to understand human behaviour requires a prior knowledge of what a person is (Oppong et al., 2023). Like Western philosophy, African philosophy has also preoccupied itself with questions about human nature and personhood (Gyekye, 1978; Wingo, 2017). This fundamental question of the nature of a person is a philosophical question that is foundational to all human sciences (Ajei & Myles, 2019; Roughley, 2021) and one that conceptually and empirically connects philosophy to psychology (Oppong, 2019b). Therefore, there cannot not be a meaningful IPA or AP without a connection to African philosophy.

To attempt to showcase how IPA stands to benefit from a closer collaboration with African philosophy, I collaborated with two colleagues, philosophers at the Department of Philosophy and Classics, University of Ghana, Legon. We set for ourselves the task of illustrating that an African philosophical concept has the potential to serve as an independent theoretical postulate of explanation in IPA. We used *tiboa*, an Akan/African philosophical concept that translates into the active principle or capacity of the human mind (Oppong et al., 2023). We used *tiboa* as the theoretical postulate to explain Western psychological concepts of emotional intelligence, cognition, and personality formation. For instance, we argue that a person's *tiboa* guides them in decisions about the moral benefits of and as the source of emotional intelligence and argue that *tiboa* gives rise to emotional intelligence when properly developed in an individual (Oppong et al., 2023). Again, we also demonstrated that *tiboa* as a human quality is a person's knowledge of moral rightness and the capacity to perform actions in line with the moral compass; we then presented *tiboa* as a distinct type of long-term memory in addition to the current typology comprising declarative memory (semantic and episodic memory) and implicit memory (priming and procedural memory) (Bruck, 2020; Oppong et al., 2023). This consideration of *tiboa* as a distinct type of long-term memory challenges the current orthodoxy of an absence of a seat of moral thinking in long-term memory. We call this *morality memory* (Oppong et al., 2023). Following from morality memory, we then demonstrated that *tiboa* acts as a pivot for character formation through its ability to feel shame and used it in a monothetic approach to account for the uniformity and consistency in human nature (Oppong et al., 2023). Further, Professor Robert Serpell argues that *tiboa* is the kind of bridging construct needed to link the notion of relational personhood (*Ubuntu*) to evaluation of actual behaviour (R. Serpell, personal communication, November 17, 2023). Indeed, the foregoing discussion illustrates how IPA stands to benefit from African philosophy if IPA seeks to become a distinct, viable subfield of psychology.

3 African Cultural Anthropology as an Essential Foundation of AP

What is African cultural anthropology, and why is it of any relevance to the study of AP? Generally, cultural anthropology is conceived of as the study of living people and their cultures, noting the similarities and differences among cultural groups (Brown et al., 2020; Lowie, 1953). Nanda and Warms (2012, p. 7) put it best as 'The study of human thought, behavior, and lifeways that are learned rather than genetically transmitted and that are typical of groups of people'. In many ways, African cultural anthropology is about the study of the thoughts, behaviours, and lifeways of Africans in Africa (Nkwi, 2015). In other words, African cultural anthropology seeks to understand African cultural realities (Johnson, 2018; Owusu, 2012). I would not belabour the point that Africa and Africans have been the lifeblood of the discipline of anthropology

(Johnson, 2018; Nkwi, 2015; Owusu, 2012), as it is not the focus of this Element. I would only add that, sometimes, it appears that without Africa and the rest of the Majority World, cultural anthropology would have suffered a stunted growth (see Funk et al., 2023).

The relevance of African cultural anthropology lies in the way AP or IPA has been conceptualised. Without accentuating culture, it would be very difficult to show how AP differs from Western psychology or Asian psychology. Drawing on work done in African cultural anthropology, a distinction between Western psychology and AP has been offered. For instance, Nwoye (2015a) differentiates Western psychology from AP in that the former emphasises: (1) 'the use of objective, quantitative measuring or data gathering instruments'; (2) 'defines humans only in material, measurable, or observable terms'; (3) that human behaviour has 'no significant meaning beyond what is actually observed'; and (4) that the human mind dies with the death of the body (p. 107). On the other hand, he argues that AP tends to emphasise: (1) the connectedness of Africans to their contexts, including the invisible, such as spiritual and ancestral worlds, (2) spirituality as a key source of influence of the thoughts, behaviours, and lifeways of the living, (3) the interpreted nature of meaning of actions to self and others, and (4) that the mind and memory live on after the death of the organic human body (Nwoye, 2015a; also see Oppong, 2022). Without access to the body of knowledge in African cultural anthropology, such distinctions would have been nearly impossible to achieve formally. For instance, the current understanding that there are different developmental pathways in child development or different but equal childhoods has resulted from work in cultural anthropology and cultural psychology (Funk et al., 2023; Scheidecker et al., 2023b). Similarly, cultural psychology has benefited heavily from cultural anthropology in terms of setting the foundations and providing the methods and tools for studying people in cultural contexts (see Jahoda, 2016; Nwoye, 2020; Poortinga, 2021; Sam, 2014; Serpell, 1989, 1993).

Furthermore, African philosophy is also rooted in African cultural anthropology. Janz (2007) argues that African philosophy deals with *culturally* original questions relating to the full range of philosophical inquiry. Again, Davis (2000, p. 152) highlights Kwame Gyekye's (1939–2019) 'project of constructing the Akan life-world, in both its traditional and modern expression' and intimates that Kwame Gyekye's undertaking suggests 'the prospect of disciplinary exchange and collaboration between anthropology and philosophy'. Indeed, Kwasi Wiredu (1931–2022) acknowledges the anthropology-like approach to African philosophy in the School of African Traditional Philosophy (Wiredu, 2004) to which African philosophers like Kwame Gyekye belong. Kwasi Wiredu is often classified as an anti-traditionalist or as belonging to the anti-ethnophilosophy school along with the French-speaking

African philosopher, Paulin Hountondji (born in 1942). However, Kwasi Wiredu argues that he still disagrees with Paulin Hountondji in the sense that he recognises the anthropology-like approach to African philosophy as relevant except for the lack of critical stance often taken by some traditionalists (Wiredu, 2004). All of this provides evidence in support of the connection between African culture and African philosophy. The African anthropology–AP connection is important to highlight because it shows that African philosophy and AP tend to have a broadly similar anthropology-like approach to understanding human nature (see Oppong, 2017).

Perhaps there is no gainsaying that culture is crucial to the study of AP (see 1.2 Centrality of Culture). It was with this understanding that I previously suggested that the study of psychology in Ghana and Africa should include mandatory modules on African philosophical thought; African psychological thought: psychological implications of proverbs, wise-sayings, and ethnic cosmologies; parapsychology; history of Ghana; and sociology or anthropology of Ghana (Oppong, 2016). Specifically, I advocated for this curriculum reform, arguing that inclusion of the suggested courses in the psychology curriculum in Ghana, for instance, will expose Ghanaian psychology students to the necessary folk and philosophical psychologies required for the indigenisation or Africanisation project. Introduction of such courses should encourage Ghanaian psychologists to explore Ghanaian ethnic cosmologies to identify and describe their cognitive, affective, and behavioural processes and content to elevate folk and philosophical Ghanaian psychologies to Indigenous scientific psychology (Oppong, 2016, p. 10).

At a minimum, we recommended such books as *African Cultural Values: An Introduction* (published in 1996) by Kwame Gyekye, a renowned Ghanaian philosopher, and *Tradition and Change in Ghana: An Introduction to Sociology* (published in 2003) by G. K. Nukunya was an important introduction to developing an African or Ghanaian approach to psychology (Oppong, Asante, & Oppong, 2012; see Allwood, 2018). Other African philosophers like Kwasi Wiredu (1931–2022), Ifeanyi Anthony Menkiti (1940–2019), and John Samuel Mbiti (1931–2019) are also good sources on African philosophy, and by extension AP, as they also address 'metaphysics, epistemology, axiology, and methodology, as well as with the problems and opportunities of intercultural philosophizing' (Janz, 2007, p. 690).

However, Allwood (2018) took issue with the inclusion of parapsychology in such a curriculum for an AP. Parapsychology is said to be the study of paranormal experiences – phenomena that defy the 'boundaries of time, space and force' (Pasricha, 2011, p. 4). I tend to agree with Pasricha (2011, p. 8) that the study of parapsychology 'would enhance understanding of certain medical, psychological and psychiatric disorders that cannot be explained in terms of currently available theories of the genetic or environmental influences'. This view is consistent with the distinction between Western psychology and AP offered by Nwoye (2015a). For emphasis, I will repeat the aspects that align with this view: (1) the connectedness of Africans to their contexts, including the invisible, (2) spirituality as a key source of influence of the thoughts, behaviours, and lifeways of the living, and (3) the mind and memory live on after the death of the organic human body (Nwoye, 2015a; see Oppong, 2022). For instance, Pasricha (2011) identifies, among other things, near-death experiences and out-of-body experiences, reincarnation, past-life regression, apparition, and precognition as paranormal experiences or phenomena. These paranormal experiences align with African cosmology and spirituality as discussed earlier. For instance, among other themes, Dzokoto (2020) in her study of the Akan concept of mind, *adwen*, indicated that it was characterised as 'porosity'. As a term, Taylor (1992) used 'porosity' to contrast the Western concept of self and mind ('that recognises distinct boundaries between mind and body, self and other, physical and the cosmic') with other concepts of the mind that acknowledge it as being 'associated with a permeability, a bleeding into one another, such that the self and the other, the physical and the cosmic, and the mind and the body cross over into each other and influence each other, often with discernible phenomenological impact' (Dzokoto, 2020, p. 83). Again, she found that the Akans of Ghana attributed causality to bad people such that people with bad *adwen* can 'directly affect the physical world without physical mediation' (Dzoko, 2020, p. 83) and that 'a good *adwen* by itself is not sufficient to provide complete protection against misfortune' (Dzokoto, 2020, p. 86). This is because a good *adwen* 'neither eliminates feelings such as envy and jealousy from the minds of others, nor thwarts other dangerous motivations from others' (Dzokoto, 2020, p. 86). Such a view of the mind allows for and is consistent with a worldview that acknowledges the existence of paranormal experiences. This is also critical to African conception of mental illnesses (Asare & Danquah, 2017; Mbiti, 1969; Nwoye, 2015a, 2015b; Opare-Henaku & Utsey, 2017; Oppong, 2020a). Therefore, asking African psychology students to study parapsychology provides the opportunity to see themselves in the study of their own psychological make-up. This has the advantage of increasing the relevance of the psychology they study as well as the explanatory power of the body of psychological knowledge they obtain through the study.

A related discipline that is often ignored by AP is sociolinguistics – the study of how languages serve a community and are shaped by the social nature of the members of the community. It is also related to ethnolinguistics – a branch of anthropology. I bring this issue up for serious consideration among AP researchers and practitioners because many AP researchers and practitioners are already informally appropriating techniques from sociolinguistics (see Nwoye, 2020). That, in this Element, I have tried to analyse language as a tool to understand human beings in a context is just one example. Work by sociolinguistics should be considered for use in AP as well. For instance, Kofi Agyekum of the University of Ghana has worked on issues such Akan cultural concepts and expressions for 'stress', 'distress', 'sorrow', and 'depression' (Agyekum, 2020) as well as Akan body part expressions (Agyekum, 2018), with some of his work focusing on ethnopragmatics of Akan language usage in expressing behaviours, thoughts, and emotions. I only mention Kofi Agyekum as an example as there are likely other African sociolinguists doing similar work across the continent of Africa. Such anthropological work from the field of sociolinguistics has the potential to offer new insights into understanding behaviours, thoughts, and emotional expressions of Africans. Therefore, I will call on AP researchers to collaborate with not only African philosophers but also African sociolinguistics researchers.

4 Emerging Theoretical Contributions in AP

In this section of the Element, I attempt to present a series of theoretical contributions that have been made by Africa-based psychologists in AP or IPA. These theories have not necessarily become accepted into the canon of hegemonic psychology; however, they are important contributions from AP that need to be considered when teaching the next generation of Africa-based psychologists interested in AP or 'doing' AP as a professional psychologist in Africa. To accomplish this aim, I choose to highlight some of my own theoretical contributions first, followed by equally important contributions by other notable figures in AP. There are others, like epistemic agency and an integrated model of human actions and conditions, that I decided not to discuss here. It is worthy of note that many of my theoretical contributions have been responses to theoretical questions I posed earlier in my work that required answers; this is to say that I respond to my own questions, as I am aware that many of these questions may remain unanswered if I do not attempt to deal with them. The theoretical contributions presented here are not meant to be exhaustive but rather illustrative of the kinds of contributions being made and that will be made in the future. To use this Element to teach AP, the instructor is encouraged to consult other sources or texts on AP by eminent Africa-based psychologists pursuing AP as their subspecialty in psychology. As indicated earlier, Africa-based psychologists in so-called Western-oriented AP are not to be considered part of AP proper as defined by the four strands discussed previously (see 1.4 Strands of IPA).

4.1 Selected Theoretical Contributions by Seth Oppong

4.1.1 Biocultural Theory of Personhood

I developed the biocultural theory of personhood while undertaking a historical study on tracing the ancient history of psychology in Ghana (see Oppong, 2017). I wanted to see what existed before May 1967, when the University of Ghana established a full-blown academic Department of Psychology (Oppong, Asante, & Oppong, 2012; Oppong et al., 2014; Oppong, 2013a, 2016, 2017). This led me to explore pre-colonial texts such as a philosophical dissertation on the apathy of the human mind by an African from the present-day Republic of Ghana named Anton Wilhelm Amo (1701–84) and a colonial text on the history of present-day Ghana by an African educated in Africa and later the first moderator of the Presbyterian Church of Ghana, Carl Christian Reindorf (1834–1917). As a result of Anton W. Amo's dissertation, *On the Apathy of the Human Mind or the Absence of Sense and of the Faculty of Sensing in the Human Mind and the Presence of These in Our Organic and Living Body* (defended in 1734), and subsequent work including *A Philosophical Disputation Containing a Distinct Idea of Those Things that Belong Either to the Mind or to Our Living Organic Body* (defended by his student in 1734) and *Treatise on the Art of Philosophizing Soberly and Accurately* (published in 1738), I had crowned him the 'Father of Black Psychology', taking the crown away from Francis Cecil Sumner, the first African American to receive a Ph.D. in psychology in 1920 (Oppong, 2017). It was within this context that the biocultural theory of personhood emerged.

This theory is based on the ethnopsychological perspectives of the Akan people of Ghana and, to a greater extent, La Côte d'Ivoire, all in West Africa, that personhood is somewhat achieved. In other words, a human being is not at birth endowed with personhood and must instead work towards achieving this status throughout life (Oppong, 2023b). This formulation also recognises that there are certain developmental tasks or societal expectations that one must negotiate to become a person. Thus, the theory states that an individual is not born with the status of a person and must work to achieve this status by negotiating societal expectations that are age-appropriate; these expectations are deemed age-appropriate and co-determined by an interaction between the individual's physical development and society. In other words, society evaluates one's progress towards becoming a person according to one's physical development, which often crudely corresponds to chronological age (see Figure 1). I identified seven stages of becoming a person within the Akan ethnopsychology, comprising *abotafra /abofra ngee* (rendered as babyhood; 0 to 1 year), *abofra* (childhood; 1 to 7 years), *abaamuwaa/ abaayewa* (adolescence; 8 to 20 years), *aberante/ ababaawa* (young adulthood; 21 to 49 years), *abeserewa* (middle adulthood; 50

Stage	English rendition	Possible age	Developmental Tasks			
			Knowledge of good and bad (morality)	Responsibility for one's actions and inactions	Meeting one's material and immaterial needs of existence	Helping others (Prosocial behaviour)
Abotafra /Abofra ngee	Babyhood	0 – 1	Not expected	Not expected	Totally dependent on adults	Not expected
Abofra	Childhood	1 – 7	Should begin to learn about morality	Should begin learning to take responsibility but there is no high expectation	Not expected	Should begin to show early signs of this
Abaamuwaa /Abaayewa	Adolescence	8 – 24	Should show this at a matured level	Should show this at a matured level	Should begin learning skills/vocations that enable the person to fulfill this task in the future	Would be required to show this
Aberante/ Ababaawa	Young adulthood	25 – 49	Should show this at a matured level	Should show this at a matured level	Would be expected to independently carry out this task; should be married and expected to have and raise children; industriousness and engaged in some income-generating activities	Would be required to show this
Abeserewa	Middle adulthood	50 – 70	Should show this with wisdom	Should show this with wisdom	Would be expected to independently carry out this task; should preparing to disengage from active physical or strenuous activities; should have accumulated reasonable material wealth	Would be required to show this with wisdom
Akɔkora/ Aberewa	Early late adulthood	70 – 80	Should show this with wisdom	Should show this with wisdom	Would be expected to independently carry out this task; supporting the children and others	Would be required to show this with wisdom
Akɔkora posoposo/ Aberawa posoposo	Late adulthood	81+	Should show this with wisdom	Should show this with wisdom	There is no expectation for the person to physically meet his/her material needs because of expected physical weaknesses; becomes dependent on *mmabun* (youth comprising *mmarante and mmabaawa*) and *mmeserewa* such like *mmofra* and *mmotafra*.	Would be required to show this with wisdom

Figure 1 Biocultural theory of personhood

to 69 years), *akɔkora/aberewa* (early late adulthood; 70 to 80 years), and *akɔkora posoposo/ aberawa posoposo* (late adulthood; 81+ years). In addition, I identified the following developmental tasks or societal expectations: (1) knowledge of good and bad (morality), (2) responsibility for one's actions and inaction, (3) meeting one's material and immaterial needs of existence, and (4) helping others (prosocial behaviour) (Oppong, 2023b, 2017).

I argue that this theory 'provides a more useful framework for counselling, psychotherapy on existential problems, personality assessment, curriculum development, and assessment of successful outcomes of living' (Oppong, 2017, p. 20). This is because it outlines the expected social responsibilities an individual should be able to execute for oneself and for the benefit of others in the community. This view is consistent with the concept of *tiboa* discussed earlier (Oppong et al., in press). In terms of school readiness for young children, the expectation of early childhood education, among other things, should be to develop in the children a nascent sense of morality and becoming responsible for one's actions and inactions (Oppong, 2023b, 2017). When contrasted with Nsamenang's social ontogenesis theory, I self-criticised the biocultural theory of personhood for focusing on 'the material existence of the person's journey through life on earth' (Oppong, 2023b, p. 32), ignoring the pre- and post-material existence of an individual.

4.1.2 Model of Valued Human Cognitive Abilities

The journey to develop this African theory of cognitive abilities or intelligence began in 2010 when I started teaching educational psychology at Regent University College of Science and Technology in Accra, Ghana. I had by then begun engaging with philosophical texts by Kwame Gyekye on African cultural values relating to knowledge and wisdom. I was dismayed by the lack of a coherent African theory of intelligence at the time. Fortunately, in 2017, I was lucky when Professor Robert Serpell found me through my critical work on early childhood research and practices in Africa (see Oppong, 2015a). As a result, he gifted me a copy of his book titled *The Significance of Schooling: Life-Journeys in an African Society* (published in 1993) in 2018. After studying the book, I found his ethnographic study of the conceptions of intelligences among Chewa speakers in Zambia. I began to teach his findings in my introductory psychology course at William V. S. Tubman University in Liberia. Thus, when I received an invitation from Vivian Dzokoto to contribute to a special issue on African cultural models in psychology (Serpell et al., 2022), I took advantage of the call to expand the work through a systematic review methodology to formulate what an African theory of intelligence would look like (see Figure 2). Therefore, this theory is rooted in ethnographic evidence from Africa about the conceptions of intelligence or cognitive abilities. I also drew heavily on African philosophical conceptions of cognitive abilities as well.

This theory identifies three interrelated components of cognitive abilities from an African perspective, namely: cognitive competence, wisdom, and socio-emotional competence. The understanding is that cognitive competence, in a broad sense, is similar to what Western psychologists tend to measure as intelligence. In addition, Africans recognise the role of wisdom and socio-emotional competence in the use of cognitive competence. To become a general theory of intelligence, I allude to the fact that different human societies accentuate different components in the model based on the currency and values each component holds in that particular human society (Oppong, 2020b). Due to the need for connectedness in African societies (Oppong, 2023b: also see 4.1.1 Biocultural Theory of Personhood), wisdom and socio-emotional competencies are often emphasised to the point of overshadowing cognitive competence, though the latter is still valued, whereas the individualist orientations of most

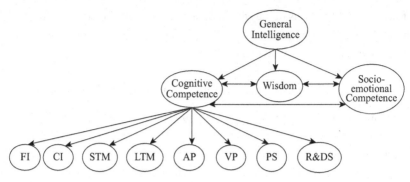

Figure 2 A model of valued human cognitive abilities

Note: FI = fluid intelligence; CI = crystallised intelligence; STM = short-term memory; LTM = long-term memory; AP = auditory processing; VP = visual processing; PS = processing speed; R&DS = reaction and decision speed.

Source: Oppong (2020b, p. 10).

Western societies lead to a de-emphasis on socio-emotional competencies and more premium being placed on cognitive competence. This may explain why Western forms of schooling emphasise analytic intelligence in what they encourage, mould, and assess in students as members of their societies.

4.1.3 Risk Chance Process Model

This theory was borne out of some work I did on occupational health psychology. When I served as an international visiting scholar at North Carolina State University, Raleigh, in 2007, I began to collect literature on occupational safety issues in the upstream oil and gas sector. It was around the time Ghana had just discovered crude oil in commercial quantities. I was then interested in pursuing a doctoral study in occupational safety in the oil and gas sector. When I returned to Ghana in 2008, I continued to work on the topic and even submitted to the late Professor Joseph Yaw Opoku of the Department of Psychology at the University of Ghana to review it for me, even though I was not formally registered as a doctoral student. When I realised that I could not register as a doctoral student, I decided to turn the work I had done on the doctoral thesis into a book (see Oppong, 2011). It was during this time I began to wonder if the existing theories of risk perceptions (i.e., protection motivation theory, risk compensation/homeostasis theory, risk preference theory, situated rationality theory, habituated action theory, social action theory, and social control theory) could explain why faulty risk perceptions lead to accidents. The extant theories of risk perceptions tended to explain why and how risk perception influences risk-taking behaviour but failed to offer any explanation as to how risk perception results in accidents.

When I became convinced by the extant theories of risk perceptions, I began to theorise around the central question and did an extensive literature review. I started by questioning the black box in the link between risk perceptions and accidents in the book to work it out in some detail for article publication in 2015 (see Oppong, 2015b). I have since then empirically tested the theories (see Oppong, 2021a).

The risk chain process simply states that an accident is more likely to result from faulty risk perceptions because faulty risk perceptions tend to lead to human error; these human errors tend to cause one to engage in risky behaviour, and the risk behaviours often result in risk exposure or exposure to hazardous conditions; once exposed to hazardous conditions, there is a higher likelihood that the risk exposure eventually leads to injuries or accidents (Oppong, 2011, 2015b, 2021a; Pheko et al., 2021; see Figure 3). It is also important to acknowledge the role of culture in determining behaviours, thoughts, and emotional expressions, including risk perceptions (see Sam, 2014). For a detailed description of the theory and its applications, consult Oppong (2015b, 2021a) and Pheko et al. (2021). An important question may relate to the African rootedness of the risk chain process model. One way to respond to this question is the claim to its African rootedness in terms of the *source* of the theoretical formulation. If we cannot divorce an idea or theory from the source and its background, it is equally possible to argue that 'Africaness' permeates the theory because the proponent is an African scholar educated solely in Africa from preschool through undergraduate to doctoral studies. Though it may not be possible to point to a particular African concept in the theories, the very idea that it is a product of an African mind – an African of the soil and by blood – operating

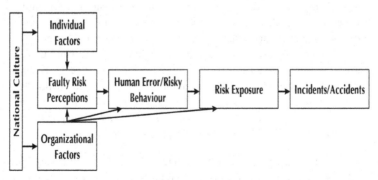

Figure 3 Risk chain process mode

Source: Oppong (2015b, p. 31).

from within West Africa and now Southern Africa should be a partial justification for its African rootedness. Perhaps an aspect of the theory that can be traced to the African source or mind is acknowledgement of the national culture as a potential influence on risk perception. A typical Western formulation tends to be decontexualised and often seeks to minimise the role of culture.

4.1.4 Sekyi Puzzle of Modernity

This may not be considered a serious theoretical contribution in its own right as it attempts to capture a conundrum that many people in the Majority World tend to encounter in the quest to indigenise knowledge. Simply put, the Sekyi puzzle of modernity is named after Kobina Sekyi (1892–1956), who is arguably among the first Africans to articulate this conundrum (Asante, 2011). He reflected the challenge of modernity as a Gold Coast (now Ghanaian) nationalist and posed it as follows: 'how to Westernize without being Westernized; how to preserve while modernizing' (Asante, 2011, p. 96). I noted that 'Our ability to resolve this puzzle will be a major breakthrough in our efforts to Africanise knowledge production in general and psychological science in particular' (Oppong, 2016, p. 8). Fortunately, I found an effective resolution of the question in S. R. B. Attoh Ahuma's (1905) *Memoirs of West African Celebrities in Europe (1700–1850)*. In this book, Ahuma (1905) argued that:

> The Gold Coast of Guinea [now Ghana] is without controversy a peculiar country, inhabited by aboriginal tribes whose manners, customs, institutions and laws dimly, but persistently, recall an advanced stage of civilization in a golden age that has long since receded into oblivion. But the landmarks are there for all that – clear, distinct and indelible ... Four centuries of contact with Europe have in no way exorcised the spirit of our ancestors, and still it defies the remotest possibility of subjugation. The more soundly and liberally the sons of the soil are educated the more readily do they acknowledge the wisdom of the fathers, the more fervently do they pray for 'Judicious training upon Native lines', and the more solemnly do they affirm that 'apart from the natives, any attempt at statesmanlike administration is doomed to failure.' ... The Gold Coast native, therefore, will invariably 'Go Fantee' ... in his intellectual evolution, and therein lies his national salvation ... To 'Go Fantee' marks the mental terminus of the Gold Coast native, and describes his ultimate reversion to the simplicity of his forebears, *sobered and matured with all that is excellent in Western civilization* (pp. 253–4; emphasis added).

The implication is that while we attempt to modernise, we should only borrow what is excellent in Western civilisation and keep the cultural values that have kept African societies alive till date. Therefore, the decision rule might be to ask whether a particular import from a Western society serves the African community for the better in the long run rather than the immediate benefits it brings. This can then be extended to psychological knowledge and praxis to pose a similar question as to whether the theories, methods, tools, and applications we borrow contain only the positive aspects without causing harm to African societies in the long run. Thus, the Sekyi puzzle of modernity becomes a tool in critical AP in general as well as a tool for critical analysis of any Western imports. In some ways, it becomes an inversion of Kwasi Wiredu's (2004) orientation to turn the critical lens on African cultural values. The Sekyi puzzle of modernity tends to expand the critical analysis bottom-up, while Wiredu's (2004) concerns takes a top-down critical stance. It is important to note that both top-down and bottom-up critical lenses are needed to understand the contemporary life of an African.

4.1.5 Epistemological Allyship

The concept of epistemological allyship (EA) was borne out of my concern that the anti-racism literature tends to blame White people for most things without any attempt to recognise the role the marginalised plays in their marginalisation. EA calls for bidirectional relationships in collaborations between academics from the Majority World (AMWs) and influential scholars in the Minority World who 'genuinely want to see another human progress rather than seeing the one in need of assistance as merely a member of a marginalized group' (Oppong, 2023a, p. 76). It recognises that to demand the currently powerful groups to relinquish their power as gatekeepers is more likely to be resisted, and that decolonisation must be understood for what it stands for and entails – tensions and political struggles for power in knowledge production. I argue that these tensions may become more manageable when both sides (the influential gatekeepers and marginalised groups) acknowledge that the demand for power from influential groups is more likely to alienate them. Again, both sides must view members of marginalised group members simply as human beings who aspire to progress and not as people who need to be saved (such as in White saviourism) or exploiting their plight to bolster one's image as a good person (such as in optical allyship). Thus, there must be a recognition of the following: (1) demand for power creates tensions, (2) members of the marginalised groups do not need saving but rather support to be independent knowledge creators, (3) to some degree, members of the marginalised groups are culpable in their marginalisation by ceding power to the privileged few, (4) members of the marginalized groups must not seek to be saved but instead seek partnership, (5) members of the marginalised groups must assert themselves in knowledge production and dissemination, and (6) true emancipation will emanate from members of the marginalised groups and not from elsewhere.

Notwithstanding, EA requires a common understanding that influential gate-keepers in knowledge production are not obligated to members of marginalised groups if they wish not to become an ally. This is because, I argue, they have a right not to be actively involved in allyship or to avoid spaces where such issues are discussed (Oppong, 2023a). Even if the non-involvement makes the world a bad place to live, they still have a right to want to destroy themselves along with others in the bad world their non-involvement creates. It is also important to note that I cannot claim to be the first to have used the term EA, per se. Starodub (2015) first used the noun phrase 'epistemological allies' to signify like-minded persons who share a general approach to theory of knowledge and knowledge production. In addition, Starodub (2015) mentioned the phrase only once as a convenient term to use in passing, perhaps to capture the idea of borrowing a critical lens from other social movements and scholarships that agree on some approaches to knowledge production. However, I use EA to refer to the process of joining forces with like-minded people to give a helping hand to those who are tackling their epistemological struggles.

Among other things, I argue that some of the ways to enact EA include mentorship (the requirement on the part of the marginalised group members is to do critical, original, and stimulating work to attract influential gatekeepers in the first place), reading and citing sources from the Majority World (the first requirement applies here as well), and funding and sub-funding. EA-based funding must involve Western scholars collaborating 'meaningfully with their AWMs to conceptualize the study and jointly draft the research proposal as well as the grant application documentation' (Oppong, 2023a, p. 79). Sub-funding can be extracted from larger funding to be offered to AMWs to support their research if their work aligns in some significant ways with the objective of the initial larger funding. For further reading, consult Oppong (2023a).

4.1.6 Oppong-Wiredu Ethical Principle

This is not a theory or concept per se, rather an application of an African philosophical principle to ethical decision-making. It was borne out of my disillusionment that, though African philosophers like Kwame Gyekye (on the Akan ethics) and Kwasi Wiredu have written extensively about ethics in the African sense, there was still no coherent African perspective on ethics in the social and behavioural sciences. The task of developing an African perspective on ethics in the social and behavioural sciences was helped by the publication of the book *A Celebration of Philosophy & Classics* (Simpson et al., 2013) as part of the

65th anniversary celebration by the University of Ghana. In the book, I found a chapter by Kwasi Wiredu titled "Are There Cultural Universals?" (Wiredu, 2013). A reading of the chapter was all I needed to be able to develop this idea into a coherent African perspective on ethics. It is important at this point to highlight the need for Africa-based psychologists interested in AP to become well read in African philosophy, as the latter can provide ready material to theorise in AP. Here, I refer to my previous work, which has been informed largely by foundations set by African philosophers; they include work on an African theory of intelligence, biocultural theory of personhood, and *tiboa* as an independent theoretical postulate, among others.

In working out his philosophy of cultural universals, Wiredu (2013, p. 100) acknowledges that the underlying mechanisms or processes of human actions may be the same 'for all humans irrespective of whether they inhabit Europe, Asia, or Africa' but also argues that cultural variations exist in how the behaviour manifests itself. This idea can be extended to ethical decision-making as being moderated by different cultural contexts (Oppong, 2019c). In addition, one can derive from his philosophical analysis that 'we ought to be more concerned about judging the morality of our conduct rather than determining the rightness or wrongness of the reasons for the particular conduct' (Oppong, 2019c, p. 24). Though Wiredu (2013) argues in favour of universalism, he prescribes a test that becomes useful in ethical decision-making in an African context. Wiredu (2013, p. 107) instructs us in the following ways to determine if an action is universal or not:

> Let us start with the following minimal premise. We assume that every human being has a concern for his or her own interests, in whatever way the concept of interest might be defined. The problem of morals arises from the fact that not everybody has a natural inclination to be concerned about the interests of others at all times in their conduct. In consideration of this, the following imperative naturally suggests itself. 'Let your conduct at all times manifest a due concern for the interests of others.' The question, of course, is: 'What is *due* concern?' I propose the following criterion. A person may be said to manifest due concern for the interests of others if in contemplating the impact of his actions on their interests, she puts herself imaginatively in their position, and having done so, is able to welcome that impact ... If phrased as an imperative, it might be called the *principle of sympathetic impartiality* (first emphasis in the original and second emphasis added).

African societies tend to thrive on social relations such that what qualifies as morally right often translates into actions that promote community welfare, solidarity, and harmony. The implication is that the *principle of sympathetic impartiality* is teleological or consequentialist as it evaluates the results (teleological) or the impact (consequential) of an individual's actions as opposed to the actions themselves (deontological). Therefore, the *Oppong-Wiredu ethical principle* is informed by the Wireduian principle of sympathetic impartiality that acts as a golden rule for ethical decision-making. This ethical principle states that, in order to act ethically, one must at all times allow their conduct to manifest a *due concern* for other people's interests by putting themself imaginatively in their stead and, having done so, determine if they are able to welcome that impact of the action on oneself. I have applied this principle to show cultural relativity in ethical decision-making as this is not informed by a justice perspective nor a care perspective (Oppong, 2019c). This principle has also been applied to ethical dilemma cases in clinical psychology, medical, and industrial/ organisational psychology practices. Sometimes, the ethical action may be consistent with the results of justice-based ethical decision-making. However, the reasons for arriving at the decision are completely different in the African context (Oppong, 2019c).

4.1.7 Tiboa *as an Independent Theoretical Postulate*

I have already discussed, in some detail, the theoretical formulation of *tiboa* as an independent theoretical postulate in AP; therefore, I will refer readers to the aforementioned discussion (see section 2 African Philosophy as an Essential Foundation). However, I will add here that, as an independent theoretical postulate, it can be extended to explain other behaviours, thoughts, and emotions in the African context in addition to mainstream concepts such as emotional intelligence and long-term memory. In addition, *tiboa* has potential applications in applied AP. For instance, we suggest the following: (1) the construction of a Strength of *Tiboa* Scale (S*T*S) based on further exploration by both African philosophers and psychologists, (2) the use of the S*T*S in emotional intelligence research and studies on civility, honesty, ethical leadership, organisational citizenship behaviours, prosocial behaviours, organisational commitment, corporate social responsibility, counterproductive work behaviours, corruption, social deviance, studies examining effects of *tiboa* on common mental health problems and a host of others, (3) clinicians using S*T*S to screen clients who present signs and symptoms of non-psychotic disorders to establish the degree of agency and will to change or undergo or compete therapy, (4) developing *tiboa* concepts into a *Tiboa* Exploration and Animation Therapy (*T*EAT) to assist practitioners to explore and identify 'misalignments' in the *tiboa* while engaging in activities that can animate (give vigour or move to action) or give reasons for the *tiboa* to want to change and/or maintain the momentum to change, and (5) use of *T*EAT-based modalities to encourage health-promoting behaviours. Given that promoting social harmony involves recognition of one's responsibility to and natural membership of society, it stands to reason that applying *T*EAT-informed practices should encourage members of a community to ensure their physical health status as such a state implies an acknowledgement of one's duty to those who depend on them; this is to say, good health is necessary for one's ability to offer needed support to others (Oppong et al., 2023). In this regard, *T*EAT-informed interventions would be very useful for health promotion campaigns and combating public health emergencies such as the COVID-19 pandemic. For example, getting the public to understand that their good health is a public good to those who depend on them is more likely to cause them to take preventive precautions against public health emergencies. This is not to say that there might not be a possibility for psychological reactance – the 'unpleasant motivational arousal that emerges when people experience a threat to or loss of their free behaviors', which 'serves as a motivator to restore one's freedom' (Steindl et al., 2015, p. 205). That is to say, *T*EAT-informed interventions are more likely to be effective tools for health promotion if the health emergencies are presented as a threat to the freedom to provide for persons who depend on the target group and that working collectively to eliminate the threat serves everyone, including their dependents. Thus, taking public health precautions will be seen as helping themselves and their dependents as well.

I will now turn my attention to theoretical contributions from other eminent Africa-based psychologists specialising in AP. I will start with Augustine Nwoye, then discuss Augustine Bame Nsamenang's theory and Stephen Baffour Adjei's contribution. Further, I present an integrated theory of personhood to guide future work in AP based on my own work, Nwoye, Nsamenang, and other relevant empirical work on personhood in Africa.

4.2 Augustine Nwoye's Africentric Theory of Human Personhood

The basic premise of Augustine Nwoye's Africentric theory of human personhood does not depart from my theory of personhood – that 'mature human beings are not born but made' (Nwoye, 2017a, p. 42). In his seminal work on personhood, Nwoye (2017a) identified seven basic assumptions of the African worldview and five sources of human motivations. He then added an African perspective on human growth and development and two resources and processes for cultivating personhood in Africa (Nwoye, 2017a).

In terms of the seven basic assumptions of the African worldview, Nwoye (2017a) outlines the following: (1) the earth is a visible physical world inhabited by living beings or created things whereas the spiritual world is the invisible that serves as the home of the spirits, comprising 'the divinities, ancestral and ghost spirits, clan deities and other unknown invisible evil forces' (p. 47); (2) there is an interpenetration between the visible and invisible worlds in the African worldview and both worlds can communicate through facilitated perception (divination and dreaming) as well as through other rituals; (3) there are good and evil spirits as well as human beings in the universe; (4) there is a recognition of mystical causality in the universe (also see Dzokoto, 2020); (5) a well-bred African child is one that exudes 'patience, perseverance, due discretion, ability to live for others or the spirit of *Ubuntu*, obedience to parents and respect to elders, and modesty and industriousness' (p. 48); (6) there is a recognition of a genetic basis of one's personhood in Africa; and (7) there is an understanding that one's life is a multidimensional project aimed at achieving maximum success in all aspects of life – that is, the social, material, educational, and religious/spiritual aspects of life (also see Osei-Tutu et al., 2018).

Nwoye (2017a) enumerates the following as the major sources of motivation among Africans: (1) protection against shame, (2) aspiration to achieve status of respect within one's community regardless of the limitations of one's birth or background, (3) being at par with one's age-mates in life achievements, (4) avoiding incurring the wrath of one's ancestors, and (5) show of due concern for community needs and investment in social support. He further argues that human personhood development is influenced by cultural practices, including cultural socialisation processes, traditions and customs, and ritual practices, and that 'one sign of a mature or fully realized person is the ability to control one's tongue' or use silence as a means of power and courage (Nwoye, 2017a, p. 55). With respect to the resources and processes for cultivating personhood in Africa, he argues that instruments of promotion such as direct instruction, peer modelling, and 'responsibilisation' provide a process by which a child is gradually trained 'to step into adult roles as early in life as possible' through such activities as running errands and participating in household chores (Nwoye, 2017a, p. 57). This then calls into question the broad Western conceptions of child labour, including normal household chores and age-appropriate assistance provided on the farm in African contexts. This is because it is simply part of responsibilisation process. This process is found in the biocultural theory of personhood (see 4.1.1 Biocultural Theory of Personhood) and Nsamenang's social ontogenesis theory (see 4.5 Nsamenang's Social Ontogenesis Theory). In addition, there are multiple agents for promoting or cultivating human personhood in Africa, including one's biological parents, siblings, extended family members, non-sibling older children, and older adults of the community (Nwoye, 2017a). This naturally leads to developing of multiple attachments to different agents of socialisation hinged upon multiple social partners taking care of a child in the African context (see Funk et al., 2023; Oppong & Strader, 2022; Scheidecker, Boyette et al., 2023b).

4.3 Augustine Nwoye's Africentric Typology of Dreams

Using multiple, asynchronous methods for collecting data, Nwoye (2017b) set out to outline the typology of dreams in Africa. He employed four sources of data in his study of dreams, comprising (1) narrative accounts of the dreams by others than those participating in the study, (2) literature review, (3) interview data from previous research with a traditional medicine doctor, and (4) applicable anecdotal records from anthropological studies in Africa. The narrative accounts of dreams were collected among graduate students at the University of Jos (from 1987 to 1996) and Kenyatta University (from 1997 to 2008). This implies that he pulled data from different sources separated by time and space for the purposes of data triangulation. Nwoye (2017b) concluded that

> African dreams can originate from (a) within an individual in the human world (as understood in the West); (b) from other human beings in contact with other beings and realities from outside the human world on behalf of other persons ... or (c) through contact with members of the ancestral world or the world of the recently dead ... ; and (d) from the intervention of the god of medicine and other assorted patron spirits in the numinous or spiritual realm (p. 14).

Further, Nwoye (2017b) integrated the typologies reflective of African dreams based on his analysis with the Euro-American conception of dreams. These resulted in three broad typologies of dreams consisting of (1) individuocentric dreams comprising (a) compensatory dreams and (b) anticipatory dreams; (2) intersubjective dreams, and (3) transcendental/ vertical dreams (Nwoye, 2017b). Individuocentric dreams are dreams about the dreamer and relate to daily residue or the needs and concerns of the person; the compensatory subtype refers to dreams that relate to fulfilment of wishes to respond to some needs and challenges being experienced by the individual (e.g., a poor person dreaming about being rich), while anticipatory dreams concern 'the attempt to help the dreamer have a kind of symbolic/imaginative realization of what he or she consciously yearns for, and concretely [has] seen fulfilled in other people's lives' (Nwoye, 2017b, p. 9). Intersubjective dreams are dreams about the life and concerns of another person, whereas transcendental/ vertical dreams are 'a visitation or as a transcendental intervention, orchestrated through a meeting during sleep or trance, between the dreamer and a specific agent of the ancestral or the spiritual world' (Nwoye, 2017b, p. 11).

4.4 Augustine Nwoye's Africentric Paradigm to Clinical Diagnosis and Treatment

Nwoye (2015b) set out to distinguish between the notions of psychopathology in Western hegemonic psychology and AP as well as the inadequacies of the Western orthodoxy and models of psychopathology to introduce – arguably to propose – an Africentric paradigm to illness and healing. He outlines the three principal assumptions that underlie Western orthodoxy in psychopathology, namely: (1) an allopathic or biomedical model in which mental illnesses are understood to originate from pathology in the patient's anatomy and nervous system, (2) an intrapsychic theory of psychopathology whereby psychological abnormalities are understood to result from disturbances in an individual's thoughts, giving rise to irrational thoughts (including beliefs, biases, assumptions, and fears), which tend to influence a person's behaviour, and (3) a social–cultural model of psychopathology that views 'psychopathology as a product of stressful life-worlds or social contexts in which people live and work' (Nwoye, 2015b, p. 307). He acknowledges that these assumptions are valid to a greater extent and apply to the African context as well but adds 4) a spiritualist perspective based on African spirituality to account for the origin of certain instances of mental illness (Nwoye, 2015b; also see Asare & Danquah, 2017; Dzokoto, 2020; Mbiti, 1969; Nwoye, 2015a; Opare-Henaku & Utsey, 2017; Oppong, 2020a). Thus, there are four key assumptions that underlie an Africentric model of psychopathology as enumerated earlier. I have also referred to the Africentric model of psychopathology as a *biopsychotheosocial model* (as opposed to a biopsychosocial model) to be understood as an approach to treatment or an explanatory system which considers and emphasises, where applicable, any combination of the four interacting dimensions to well-being or behaviour, for example, biological, psychological, theological, and social (Oppong, 2017, p. 35). I did not use 'theological' to mean Christian theology or Islamic theology per se but to capture African spirituality in all its shapes and shades. To be fair to Nwoye (2015b), he also calls this model the 'Bio-Psycho-Social-Spiritualist (BPS-S) model'. Asare and Danquah (2017) have also similarly called this perspective the 'Biopsychosocial(s) model', where the 's' represents spiritual practice.

Based on these four assumptions, Nwoye (2015b, p. 310) then presents his Africentric paradigm to clinical diagnosis and treatment as referring to 'the interventive action that is taken to determine the source of a difficult illness', the need of which 'arises in the face of a sudden or difficult illness that refuses to remit after all medicines (including Western hospitalization) have been administered'. Therefore, clinical diagnosis should commence with the understanding that sudden psychological illnesses are instances of symbolic rather than ordinary experiences and are messages being transmitted to the relatives or family members of the client (Nwoye, 2015b). Therefore, the mental health professional ought to identify the import and content of such a symbolic message to find a proper solution and a cure to the presenting illness of the client (Nwoye, 2015b). The implication is that sudden and severe psychological illnesses should be viewed 'as meta-communications to be "read" and interpreted, rather than to be categorized or classified as emphasized in the Western Diagnostic and Statistical Manual of Mental Disorders (DSM-5)' (Nwoye, 2015b, p. 310). Thus, clinical diagnosis of sudden, severe, psychological illnesses consists of instrumental divination (a means of verification and communication by interpreting the actions of objects and other entities in relation to a certain performance or ritual) and mediumistic divination (a means of verification and communication through a spokesperson on behalf of a higher being). Regardless of the method used, divination is a skilled process of uncovering the hidden cause of a given mental illness, be it the wrath and demands of ancestors or other spiritual agencies (Nwoye, 2015b). He concludes that mental health professionals need to recognise that there are other possible nosologies for understanding sudden and severe psychological illnesses other than the DSM-5 (Nwoye, 2015b). Thankfully, an alternative nosology exists – the Azibo Nosology II (Azibo, 2014). However, this nosology deals more with the psychiatric diagnosis of personality disorders peculiar to Africa-descended people, often resulting from the psychological misorientation that centuries of enslavement, colonisation, and apartheid have left behind in Black people, though these practices have long been officially stopped (2019a).

In my view, he stops short of recommending how divination can be integrated into mainstream nosology. Nwoye's Africentric paradigm to clinical diagnosis and treatment speaks more to moderate to severe chronic mental illnesses like psychosis. Therefore, I have argued that the truth status of the belief that spirituality is a cause of mental disorders is not what is important as it does not matter anyway to the African (Oppong, 2020a). Rather, what appears to be important is incorporating the understanding of spiritual causes of sudden and severe mental illnesses into clinical practice by accommodating the beneficial consequences of motivating Africans to engage in spirituality's associated therapeutic rituals. Though African mental health professionals will not be trained in divination or become skilled at it, they ought to be willing to allow clients to seek meaning from other sources as this has a cathartic effect for the clients – a form of closure as to why something is happening to them or their relatives. The clients often want a reasonable explanation for what may be happening to them, and if it is divination that provides the best and most reasonable explanation to the client, African mental health professionals should allow the client to receive such an explanation. In this process, the mental health professional will have to 'acknowledge this belief without devaluing it while using this belief to encourage adherence to treatment' and, perhaps, offer to 'collaborate with trustworthy faith-based healers who are trained to deploy this belief to encourage adherence to treatment' by the mental health professionals (Oppong, 2020a, p. 469). It is important to make a distinction here: it is one thing to know a reasonable cause for an illness and another to prescribe an effective treatment. The implication is that it may not matter what the suspected cause of the illness may be, but a treatment is required nonetheless, suggesting that explanation and treatment can somehow be separated or one can still present multiple explanations that inform a set of treatments. Similarly, Asare and Danquah (2017) recommend the following:

> Health education on scientific causes of illness cannot eliminate spiritual belief in Africans, especially about the Belief in the Creator, Almighty God ... Clinicians utilising the Western medical practice ... should accept the belief of African clients and utilise these beliefs to increase their compliance and adherence to scientific medical treatment. Clinicians should strengthen [the] spiritual beliefs of clients who already exhibit these spiritual beliefs and direct them to use the belief positively to improve their illness and healthcare. Also, the belief can be guided by clinicians to help in illness recovery; for example, a client can be directed to modify spiritual practices (such as fasting) until he/she recovers from illness. Spiritual healers should be acknowledged in the healthcare practice in Africa. The Spiritual healers should be trained to understand basic medical conditions in order for them to modify spiritual practices to the needs of the client; for example suspending clients' fasting when they are ill (p. 3).

Thus, the following can be recommended: (1) collaboration between mental health professionals and faith-based healers for a cross-referral system, (2) training of professionals in the understanding of both allopathic and African paradigms to disease and disease management for a common frame of reference, (3) recognition of the therapeutic effects of rituals used by faith-based healers, and (4) the patient's rights being extended to include the right to seek multiple but less conflicting treatments at the same time. After all, most African clients with sudden and severe mental illnesses tend to seek herbal treatment, followed by spiritual and allopathic, in that order (Asare & Danquah, 2017).

It is worth noting that Augustine Nwoye's epistemological positioning seems to reflect the recommendation given by S. R. B. Attoh Ahuma (1905) to resolve the Sekyi puzzle of modernity: that Africans will invariably go indigenous in their intellectual evolution, and therein lies their epistemic authenticity and restoration (also see Oppong, 2019a). Therefore, to go indigenous implies a mental break with prior Western influence and 'the ultimate reversion to the simplicity of our forebears, sobered and matured with all that is excellent in Western civilization' (Ahuma, 1905, p. 254). This is because in both his Africentric typology of dreams (2017b) and the key assumptions of psychopathology in his Africentric model of psychopathology (Nwoye, 2015b), Nwoye integrates useful Western knowledge applicable to Africans with original African perspectives. This stance also takes seriously the caution by Mpofu (2002, p. 181) that 'human societies and cultures have similarities as well as differences' and that 'With modernization and globalization of the world's economies, the similarities between societies may actually increase' so that 'Some psychological theories that were developed in Western societies may increasingly become applicable to non-Westerners'. For instance, most Western-educated Africans and urbanised Africans tend to live a life closer to that of the members of Western societies but that are still different in many ways (Bandura, 2018; Jukes et al., 2021; Keller, 2016; Oppong & Strader, 2022). Keller (2016) describes Western-educated and urbanised Africans operating in an autonomous relatedness mode, while less educated rural Africans operate in a hierarchical relatedness mode. Western-educated Africans and urbanised Africans tend to differ from less educated rural Africans in terms of their sense of autonomy being higher than the latter group (a quality that makes them closer to members of Western societies). However, they differ from members of Western societies in terms of their retention of the quality of relatedness or collectivism or communalism (Oppong & Strader, 2022). Augustine Nwoye's epistemological positioning also is consistent with my own view that current psychological knowledge is valid to the extent that it helps largely to explain the thoughts, behaviours, and emotional expressions of some groups of humans (i.e., members of Western societies) – although the minority – and our quest to indigenise does not mean uncritical rejection or acceptance of Western orthodoxy but rather working to expand this narrow perspective with missing perspectives so that psychology can be a truly global science (Oppong, 2022a, 2020b, 2019a, 2016).

4.5 Augustine Bame Nsamenang's Social Ontogenesis Theory

One of the earliest theoretical formulations on human development and personhood in Africa was advanced by Augustine Bame Nsamenang (1951–2018) in the early 1990s. He called it the *social ontogenesis theory*, a theory developed to advance our understanding of the lifespan development of an African child or person (Oppong, 2023b). Like my own theory about personhood (biocultural theory of personhood), he built his theory on the ethnopsychological perspectives and child-rearing practices of the Nso people in Cameroon, who viewed lifespan development as a continuum from before, during, and after life (Nsamenang, 1992, 2006). Thus, Nsamenang (1992, 2006) identified three phases of selfhood comprising a *spiritual selfhood* (a phase at or before conception and ending with the cutting of the umbilical cord), *social selfhood* (a phase beginning from birth and ending with death of the human organic body), and *ancestral selfhood* (the final phase that continues after the biological death of a person and immersion in the ancestral world). When the three phases are put together, he calls the set *human ontogenesis* (Nsamenang, 2006).

However, Nsamenang (2006) employed the term *social ontogenesis* to describe the growth and development that take place during the *social selfhood* phase. *Social selfhood* relates to the material existence of a person or the phase during which an individual delivered by the mother or by other means comes into this world and lives as a human being; this phase is said to consist of seven stages with specific developmental tasks (Louw & Louw, 2014; Nsamenang, 1992; Oppong, 2023b). These seven stages include (1) newborn; (2) social priming (pre-social and characterised by physiological markers or reflexes such as crying, sucking, smiling, etc.); (3) social apprenticeship (socialisation and responsibilisation); (4) social entrée (marked by the onset of puberty); (5) social internship (marked by preparation for adulthood including rites of passage); (6) adulthood; and (7) old age and death. A key characteristic of Nsamenang's social ontogenesis theory is that the stages within the social selfhood phase are 'marked by distinctive developmental tasks, defined within the framework of cultural realities and developmental agenda' (Nsamenang, 2006, p. 3), rather than being marked by chronological age (Louw & Louw, 2014; Nsamenang, 1992; Oppong, 2023b). Further, he argued that, as children grow, they are given opportunities to gradually learn new, valuable skills in the community through progressive assignment of different roles and scaffolding based on 'perception of their social maturity or competence' (Nsamenang, 2006, p. 4). Thus, from a human ontogenetic perspective, the human life cycle consists of nine stages comprising the spiritual selfhood, seven stages of social selfhood, and ancestral selfhood.

4.6 Stephen Baffour Adjei's Negotiated Agency and Social Intentionality of Agency

Stephen Baffour Adjei introduced the concept of negotiated agency in 2017 and expanded it to include social intentionality of agency in 2018. He developed both theoretical postulates in a study of intimate partner violence, focusing on the decision to leave or stay in abusive conjugal relationships among women in Ghana. Often, to Western observers, there is very little to understand why a woman experiencing intimate partner violence will not leave such an abusive relationship. This is partly because Western societies tend to view agency as a property of a person and constituted by individual psychological states and motives as expected in individualistic cultures or people with independent selves. Autonomy – decisions and actions that use the self as the frame of reference only or the idea of 'I, my, and me' – is valued in such Western settings (see Keller, 2016). However, Adjei (2017) found that agency is expressed differently in relational contexts in that, instead of being a property of a person, it is best to consider agency as a joint product of a kind of negotiation between individual and familial relationships and identities. Adjei (2018) further expanded the concept of negotiated agency to highlight the fact that the agency in relational contexts has social intentionality, to the extent that a person's intentional behaviour is both constituted by the individual and constrained by their embeddedness in community and family relations. Thus, it becomes a negotiation between *self-in-community* and *community-in-self*, as there cannot be a *self* without the community and a community without the *self* (see Oppong, 2023b). Thus, the concept of negotiated agency and social intentionality can be viewed as self-determination cast within the constraints of community needs and concerns – though you are free to act, you must act as if the community has allowed you to act or that the community permits you to act in a way that they accept or allow.

Does that mean there is no individual accountability at all as agency is negotiated? Gyekye (2003, p. 47) argues that 'African cultures generally recognize that the naturally social human being also has individuality, personal will and an identity that must be exercised'. Thus, in Africa, there is respect for the individuality of a person that is allowed to co-exist with respect for the community, which allows for individual responsibility (Oppong, 2023b). This means that the individual is still responsible for her or his actions as the individual negotiates their intentions and determination to act. There is an Akan saying, posed as a rhetorical question: *Enti mekasɛ kɔkum wo maame a, wobɛkum no?* (to wit: will you kill your mother because I told you to do so?). Others are: *Oketerɛ nkowe ne mmako na aporɔnkyerɛni nte ho mfifire* (to wit: a frog will sweat in place of the lizard that ate the pepper), *Obi ntɔn na kokɔbedeɛ kwa* (to wit: no one sells the hen that lays eggs for no good reason), *Edua biara si ne siberɛ wɔ kwayɛ mu* (to wit: when seen from a distance, a forest is a canopy but every tree stands on its own). All of these Akan sayings reflect the self-in-community and community-in-self conceptualisation. Oftentimes, these questions are posed to invoke a sense of individual responsibility in situations where the individual, having listened to the counsel of the community and family relations, wishes to blame them for the negative outcome of a decision or an action that they took in response to the counsel. African communities expect the individual to also weigh the merit and demerit of any suggestions they give before the individual in question takes an action. Among the Akans of Ghana, they say *wo nawote wogya ho, na wonim sɛnea ehyehye fa* (to wit: since you are the one by the fire, you are also the one who knows how hot it is). Thus, though agency is negotiated and the intentionality is social, the individual is still required to accept some responsibility for any negative outcome for failing to analyse the issues thoroughly before acting on the counsel.

This has implications for decision-making in other social settings, such as the care of a sick individual. For instance, Asare and Danquah (2017, p. 2) showed that that treatment modality sought for by a client with sudden and severe mental illness is related to 'the patient's or the family's concept of the aetiology of the illness', and, acting in line with Wiredu's (2013) request to show due concern for the interests of the other people, the individual will have to understand and yield in some ways to respond to the concerns of the family relations. Thus, the concept of negotiated agency is needed not only in intimate partner violence but also to understand generally how individuals with inter-dependent selves make decisions and act in politics, treatment choice, marriage, choice of schools, choice of residence, choice of career, corruption, and a host of other settings and issues.

4.7 Unified Theory of African Personhood

In this section of this Element, I attempt to integrate the three theories of personhood into a unified theory that benefits from the strengths and overcomes the shortcomings of each theoretical formulation. Referred to as a *unified theory of African personhood*, it is an integration of Nsamenang's human ontogenesis (1992, 2006), Nwoye's Africentric theory of human personhood (2017a), and Oppong's biocultural theory of personhood (Oppong, 2017). I shall also call this new theoretical formulation the *Nsamenang-Nwoye-Oppong theory of African personhood*. The order of the names is partly informed by years of publication and alphabetical order. I take from my theory the seven stages and the four developmental tasks, merge them with the stages of social selfhood specified by Nsamenang, and expand the resulting product to include spiritual and ancestral selfhoods; I also integrate into the product the resources and processes for cultivating personhood in Africa discussed by Nwoye. Even though I merged specific aspects of each theory, all of the other details provided under each theory complete the understanding of this unified theory. Though I include empirical work from Gavi et al. (2022) and Osei-Tutu et al. (2018), these scholars were not informed by a need to theorise about human development. Thus, though their contributions are useful, they were not originally thinking of a theory of African personhood as presented in this Element. This explains why I omitted their names in the neologism created to name this new theory.

Reading this unified theory in conjunction with the individual theories and related empirical studies will provide invaluable insight into human development issues in Africa. Therefore, I suggest the following order for discussing and learning about the unified theory of African personhood: (1) Gavi et al.'s (2022) multidimensional conception of African personhood; (2) Nwoye's (2017a) seven basic assumptions of the African worldview; (3) Nwoye's (2017a) five sources of human motivations; (4) stages of the unified theory of African personhood; and (5) Osei-Tutu et al.'s (2018) conceptions of the meaning of success. Such an order and study will enrich one's understanding of human development and formation of personhood in the African setting. Thus, there are key questions that underlie the unified theory of African personhood, namely: (1) What is a person? What is a person made of? (2) What are the basic assumptions held by Africans about the relationship between a person and the world? What are the sources of a person's motivation? (3) What does it mean to be a successful person? How do you attain that success? and (4) How does a person progress through the lifespan to attain success and to display qualities of a person in an African setting? What enables the person to progress through the lifespan? Given that I have already discussed a bit of Nwoye's theory of personhood, I will rather devote attention to Gavi et al.'s (2022) and Osei-Tutu et al.'s (2018) conceptions based on their empirical work. It is sufficient to say, at this point, that Nwoye (2017a) answers question (2) and the lifespan perspective presented in Figure 4 answers question (4).

First, Gavi et al. (2022) report that an African conception of personhood is underpinned by certain moral frames of personhood, namely that (1) a person is void without communal endowments (communal moral frame); (2) a person is endowed with divine qualities (divine moral frame); and (3) the regard for a person depends on how they relate to other members of their community (interpersonal moral frame). These moral frames then evolve into a multidimensional conception of personhood comprising (1) metaphysical, (2) normative, (3) performative, and (4) divine/spiritual dimensions. The *metaphysical* dimension relates to the fact that a necessary condition for someone to have personhood is that the individual should be basically biologically constituted or must possess a human organic body. The *normative* dimension is defined by one's moral capacity or the ability to abide by societal norms relating to the duties and obligations associated with one's role and position in society.

The *performative* dimension concerns carrying out the expected obligations to the community and therefore is the evaluative element of the personhood. The *divine/spiritual* dimension is concerned with the fact that a person should exude God-like characteristics. Therefore, to be a person, one must have an organic body, know one's obligations in life as defined by the demands of society, carry out these obligations, and display godliness in all endeavours and interactions with others. This view leads to an understanding that 'personhood is conferred based on one's contribution to promoting the well-being of others and the community in general' (Gavi et al., 2022). Thus, this answers the question: What is a person? What is a person made of?

Second, Osei-Tutu et al. (2018) discovered a multidimensional conception of success coupled with multiple pathways to success. They report four dimensions of success, including (1) social, (2) material, (3) educational, and (4) religious dimensions as well as three pathways to achieving success (divine blessings, adaptability, and striving). The *social* dimension of success is concerned with meeting social obligations and expectations such as marriage and having and caring for one's children well (social expectation); attaining positions of respect in the society through career projection and asset acquisitions (social recognition); and helping the needy in the community. The *material* dimension relates to (1) being able to meet one's basic needs, (2) attaining financial independence, (3) accumulation of material wealth consisting of having unlimited resources or multiple assets, (4) home ownership, (5) business ownership/entrepreneurship, and (6) car ownership. In terms of order of importance, wealth accumulation ranked first, followed by satisfactions of basic needs, home ownership, and business ownership. The others are not as important as the aforementioned. The *educational* dimension concerns accomplishments such as completion of formal education, pursuit of higher education, and career progression. Though career progression is a sign of success related to education, it is also a means for achieving social recognition, making it serve dual purposes. The *religious* dimension is defined by achieving goals related to religious tenets such as (1) doing God's will, (2) maintaining a good relationship with God, and (3) serving God. In terms of multiple pathways to success, Osei-Tutu et al. (2018) report that success in Africa is believed to be achieved through (1) divine blessings, (2) personal striving by overcoming difficult situations, and (3) adaptability using determination, network-ing, and openness to opportunities for success. Thus, this answers the question: What does it mean to be a successful person? How do you attain that success?

The lifespan perspective depicted in Figure 4 shows the stages a person goes through as the individual progressively works their way into becoming a successful member of society who, conscious of their obligation, can meet those obligations to their family and community. During the phase of social

Left-margin annotations for the "Stages" column:

Social Selfhood

Resources and d processes for cultivating personhood, including direct instruction, peer modelling, and responsibilization.

1) Instruments for promoting personhood, including direct instruction, peer modelling, and responsibilization.
2) Multiple agents for promoting or cultivating human personhood, including biological parents, siblings, extended family members, non-sibling older children, and older adults of the community and the community at large.

Stages	Possible age	Developmental Tasks			
		Knowledge of good and bad (morality)	Responsibility for one's actions and inactions	Meeting one's material and immaterial needs of existence	Helping others (Prosocial behaviour)
Spiritual Selfhood					
Babyhood or Newborn	0 – 1	Not expected	Not expected	Totally dependent on adults	Not expected
Childhood and time for social priming and part of social apprenticeship	1 – 7	Should begin to learn about morality	Should begin learning to take responsibility but there is no high expectation	Not expected	Should begin to show early signs of this
Adolescence as a stage for full-blown social apprenticeship, social entrée, and social internship	8 – 24	Should show this at a matured level	Should show this at a matured level	Should begin learning skills/vocations that enable the person to fulfil this task in the future	Would be required to show this
Young adulthood and advanced forms of social internship	25 – 49	Should show this at a matured level	Should show this at a matured level	Would be expected to independently carry out this task; should be married and expected to have and raise children; industriousness and engaged in some income-generating activities	Would be required to show this
Middle adulthood	50 – 70	Should show this with wisdom	Should show this with wisdom	Would be expected to independently carry out this task; should preparing to disengage from active physical or strenuous activities; should have accumulated reasonable material wealth	Would be required to show this with wisdom
Late adulthood	70 – 80	Should show this with wisdom	Should show this with wisdom	Would be expected to independently carry out this task; supporting the children and others	Would be required to show this with wisdom
Old age and death	80+	Should show this with wisdom	Should show this with wisdom	There is no expectation for the person to physically meet his/her material needs because of expected physical weaknesses; becomes dependent on *mmabun* (youth comprising *mmarante* and *mmabaawa)* and *mmeserewa* such like *mmofra* and *mmotafra.*	Would be required to show this with wisdom
Ancestral Selfhood					

Figure 4 Lifespan perspective of the Nsamenang-Nwoye-Oppong theory of African personhood

Source: Author's construct.

selfhood, the individual must progressively work toward the highest expressions of each of the following developmental tasks, namely: (1) knowledge of the societal moral code, (2) ownership of responsibility for one's actions and inaction, (3) satisfaction of one's material and immaterial needs of existence, and (4) performance of prosocial behaviours. Determination of the nature of the developmental task expected to be expressed by an individual depends on the perception of a person's physical development (i.e., often corresponding to one's age, reflecting a belief in the biological basis/preparedness for human development in Africa), social maturity, or competence. To assist the individual in going through the lifespan, there are some resources and processes to guide the person to cultivate a capacity for the highest expression of personhood defined by the community (dimensions of success and pathways), including: (1) such processes as direct instruction, peer modelling, and responsibilisation through (2) multiple agents such as one's biological parents or guardians, siblings, extended family members, peers, older adults of the community, and the community at large.

On a related note, I need to address a concern, though not a negative one, raised by Allwood (2018) that 'It seems that what Oppong is looking for here is the development of research on what is common to all persons with almost any kind of connection to Africa' (p. 27). I may not have considered AP in this sense, as African metaphysics recognises and values individuality amid promoting communalism (Gyekye, 2003; Oppong, 2023b). Although the unified theory of African personhood is one that may not be applicable to all Africans, by and large, the theory demonstrates the possibility of developing theories and concepts that can apply to many Africans, thus addressing the concern raised by Allwood (2018). The question of limited application of theories also applies to theories in hegemonic psychology in Western contexts as well. Jovanović (2005, p. 78) alleges that internationalisation of psychology is asymmetrical such that it seeks 'to promote, distribute or impose psychological knowledge of a very specific Western territorial and cultural origin to the other parts of the world territory and socio-cultural landscape'. Thus, Western psychology also has a similar challenge when marginalised sections of this broad categorisation turn the critical lens onto itself. In sum, it is my hope that this unified theory of African personhood will be taught in developmental psychology classes across Africa.

5 African Philosophy of Science and Research Methodology

When I began this section of this Element, I wanted to describe specific empirical studies in AP that showcase the different methodological approaches taken to collect and analyse data. However, I found a better way to present this section by focusing on common approaches themselves and sharing examples as I discuss each approach. First, I will focus on research design issues, followed by data collection methods and data analysis methods used. The examples of studies using AP-informed research methods are not meant to be exhaustive but rather illustrative. Before diving into the specific methodological issues, I will speak broadly about the philosophy of science with respect to AP.

Elsewhere, I have argued for recognition of the fact that philosophy of science is important to training psychologists to theorise (Oppong, 2014, 2022b), particularly for AP. Experimentation in psychology has also been criticised by Jahoda (2016). Therefore, I will not deal with such issues here. Rather, I will deal generally with what might constitute a reasonable philosophy of science for AP. Nwoye (2022) has suggested that AP should pursue (1) an epistemology of open philosophy of psychology and selective pluralism, (2) a philosophy of constructive alternativism, and (3) multiple epistemologies or other ways of knowing. In mainstream philosophy of science, this will translate into postmodernist philosophy coupled with pragmatism. In other words, practitioners and researchers in AP should recognise that (1) there are different ways of obtaining valid knowledge (epistemologies) and (2) we must be pragmatic in our orientation and not hold a particular allegiance to any sides of the philosophical debates (i.e., be willing and confident to project alternative ways of obtaining knowledge even if it is likely to be faced with criticism or backlash).

In agreement with Nwoye (2022), I have argued previously, on an ontological level, that there is an urgent need for researchers from Majority World settings, including AP researchers, to become open to a discipline that:

> encourages 'plura-versalims' (sic) or 'multi-versalism' ... [and] recognizes relative truths. This then compels the non-western scholar to view imported truths from western scholars as other interpretations and evaluate them accordingly. Following from this ontological position of 'multiversal' realities, non-western scholars should adopt a positivist-hermeneutic philosophy and axiological position that seeks to incorporate their endogenous paradigms or ethno-philosophies ... The purpose is to ensure that the 'hermeneutic' element of the positivist-hermeneutic orientations derives from the 'local' instead of a non-existing 'global' worldview (Oppong, 2014, p. 251).

Generally, the ontological positioning depicted in the preceding quote then reflects the calls for epistemic disobedience among African scholars (Chilisa, 2019; Mignolo, 2018; Nwoye, 2022; Oppong, 2019a). I further argue that 'the oppositions between realism and idealism on one hand and positivism and interpretivism on the other are needless', as each of these contrasting positions has its own strengths and shortcomings (Oppong, 2014, p. 252). Arguing from the communal nature of Africans (several references have been made to this notion already in this Element), Chilisa (2019) referred to the African philosophy of science in terms of *relational ontology* (i.e., negotiated reality achieved through social construction of realities), *relational epistemology* (i.e., knowledge as something socially constructed by people with connections to other people and their environment, improving the knowledge they receive and creating new meanings as a result), and *relational axiology* (i.e., research guided by principles of responsibility, respectful representation, reciprocal appropriation, and obligations; therefore, research cannot be value-free). African philosophy of science is relational because of the social embeddedness of the African (Gyekye, 2003; Oppong, 2023b). It is particularly important to recognise that 'African speech reflects both personal and community viewpoints' as, often, the African 'introjects – unconsciously absorbing aspects of external reality into the self – to ventriloquate' (Oppong, 2020b, pp. 33–4). Samuelson (2009, p. 52) defines ventriloquation as 'when a speaker speaks through the voice of another for the purpose of social or interactional positioning'. The epistemological sequelae from this multiversal ontology is constructivism, while the axiological positioning relates to embracing a science that does not deny the place of value and subjectivity. The methodological result is a qualitative research approach and mixed-methods approach (Chilisa, 2019; Nwoye, 2022; Oppong, 2014, 2019a; Oppong Asante & Oppong, 2012).

5.1 Ethnographical and Other Qualitative Methods

As already gathered from the ontological and epistemological positioning of prominent scholars in AP, the widely used research design in AP is qualitative methods including ethnography. There appears to be no point in trying to deal with the definition, scope, and steps involved in ethnography or qualitative research methods, as a lot has been written on these topics. You may consult Chilisa's (2019) *Indigenous Research Methodologie*s or relevant chapters in Nwoye's (2022) *African Psychology: The Emergence of a Tradition*, particularly chapters four, five, and eleven. Both Chilisa (2019) and Nwoye (2022) provide guidance on the use of qualitative data collection tools such as interviews and focus group discussions. Examples of AP-related studies that have used qualitative research methods include Serpell's (1993) study of intelligence of Chewa speakers in Zambia; Nwoye's (2017b) study of the type and content of dreaming in Africa; Dzokoto's (2020) study of the Akan theory of the mind; Osei-Tutu et al.'s (2018) study on meanings of success among Ghanaians; Gavi et al.'s (2022) study of conceptions of personhood in Ghana; Appiah et al.'s (2021) work exploring the experiences of rural adults in Ghana who participated in a group-based positive psychology intervention programme; and Wissing et al. (2020), who also used a similar approach to study motivations for relationships as sources of meaning among Ghanaian and South Africans. Again, Osei-Tutu et al. (2020) used a qualitative approach to explore conceptions of well-being based on four Ghanaian languages. Currently, I am also leading a team to carry out a study on Indigenous knowledge about child-rearing practices in rural Malawi and Zambia (commissioned by Firelight Foundation) using a qualitative approach where interviews and focus group discussions have already been conducted. In addition, I am leading the same team to conduct document review and analysis on childcare conditions in rural Malawi and Zambia, where the reports on community-generated data are being analysed using content analysis.

Serpell's (1993) study was an ethnographic one, while the others were more regular qualitative studies using individual interviews. It is important to high-light that there are not too many ethnographic studies in AP. This may be because ethnography utilises an anthropological research methodology, 'a skill that is often lacking among psychologists', with AP researchers being no exception, while, at the same time, such a methodology is very time-consuming (Oppong, 2020b, p. 6). Perhaps this calls for proper training in anthropological research methodology to equip the next generation of AP researchers and practitioners with the skill they will need to take AP to the next level. After all, many of the leading AP researchers were never formally trained in anthropological research methodology and had to learn on their own. Therefore, the trial-and-error era of deploying anthropological methodology for the benefit of AP should end with formal training in decolonised anthropological research methodology. A good start will be Chilisa's (2019) *Indigenous Research Methodologies* for AP researchers.

5.2 Mixed-Methods Design

Mixed methods is another approach used in AP research. Chilisa (2019) and Nwoye (2022) deals with this topic in some detail. I refer to Nwoye's (2022) support for an epistemology of open philosophy of psychology and selective pluralism as well as my own advocacy for multiversal ontology and the resulting epistemology and axiology. Based on such references, I argue that the use of a mixed-methods approach ensures that strengths and shortcomings of qualitative and quantitative approaches are balanced out. Chilisa (2019) argues for a decolonised mixed-methods approach so that the African researcher is not held captive by any particular mainstream method (on either side of the debate) or those accepted in the canon of knowledge in the given social science discipline. The mixed-methods approach is not used at the same scale as qualitative research methods, though the former still features as a common useful method in AP research. For instance, Noyau and Gbeto (2004) used a mixed-methods approach to study the conceptions of intelligence among Ewe speakers in the Republic of Togo, where they employed semantic analysis of the Ewe language through an interview and administration of a questionnaire developed based on the interviews. Similarly, Grigorenko et al. (2001) used a sequential exploratory mixed-methods design where they conducted ethnographic study followed by a quantitative study. In their study, they sought to explore conceptions of intelligence among Luo speakers in rural Kenya and to examine interrelations among these various components of Luo conceptions of intelligence as they are applied to real-world individuals via both the indigenous conception and Western assessments of intelligence as well as measures of school achievement (Grigorenko et al., 2001). I have also used a mixed-methods approach in indigenous occupational health (Oppong, 2018, 2021b).

In that study, I used interviews, a focus group discussion, and observations as part of the qualitative phase of study to develop indigenous road symbols and a risk perception scale, whereas the quantitative phase involved testing comprehension of both standard road signs and the indigenous equivalents for comparison to determine which sets of symbols enhance comprehension and reduce the risk of road accidents (Oppong, 2018, 2021b).

5.3 Systematic Review Methodology

Perhaps a good place to start a discussion on a systematic review methodology is whether it is even a research methodology and not just a literature review. A systematic review methodology uses a set of protocols such as the Preferred Reporting Items for Systematic Reviews and Meta-Analyses (PRISMA) protocol. It is considered to offer arguably the best or highest form of evidence in the evidence hierarchy, over and above randomised controlled trials (Laher & Hassem, 2020; Oppong, 2020b; Russell et al., 2009). It has served as the basis for developing standards of practice or care in medicine, nursing, and other health professions (Laher & Hassem, 2020; Oppong, 2020b; Russell et al., 2009). However, the quality of the results of a systematic review methodology depends on the quality of the individual studies making up the sample of studies. Unfortunately, this approach has not been extensively used by AP researchers, particularly for theorising. This is not to say that Africa-based researchers are not using a systematic review methodology at all. It is being used, but not from a relational African philosophy of science. In addition, most Africa-based psychologists who use a systematic review methodology will not identify as AP researchers in any sense. I used a systematic review methodology in the development of the African theory of intelligences by pooling together the existing evidence about implicit theory of intelligences among Africans (Oppong, 2020b). It is my hope that AP researchers will embrace a systematic review methodology to expand their repertoire of methods and tools. I have already cautioned that African researchers should allow the problems they study to dictate the methods that are applicable and useful to study the research problems (Oppong, 2013b). For guidance on how to undertake systematic reviews, interested AP researchers can consult Laher and Hassem (2020). Laher and Hassem (2020) developed their guidelines for conducting systematic reviews by considering the peculiarities in conducting psychological research in Africa.

5.4 Data Sources and Analysis

Often, AP researchers think of their primary source of data as the individual respondents. By this, I mean that the people about whom the study is being conducted are assumed to be the major source of data for the study. While I am not downplaying this notion, I wish to also state that there can be other sources of data. One such source of data is African proverbs. They encapsulate abstractions of reflections and observations about human nature passed on orally within a community. For instance, Dzokoto et al. (2018) used Akan proverbs as a source of data to explore norms, display rules, and regulation of emotions among Akans of Ghana. Unlike many other ethnic groups in Africa, a compendium of 7,015 Akan proverbs has been compiled by and published by Appiah et al. (2007), *Bu Me Bɛ* (title of the compendium), making it easier for those interested in studying African proverbs to do so. It is by far the largest and most comprehensive published compendium of Ghanaian proverbs, with the first compendium (Christaller, 1879) having only half as many. This compendium has the original proverbs in the Akan language, English renditions, and their interpretations in English (Appiah et al., 2007). In situations where there is no published compendium of proverbs, one can still utilise qualitative data collection methods to collect proverbs for analysis.

As previously stated, Nwoye (2017b) studied content and types of dream among Africans using four sources of data, namely: (1) narrative accounts of the dreams by others than those participating in the study, (2) literature review, (3) interview data from previous research with a traditional medicine doctor, and (4) applicable anecdotal records from anthropological studies in Africa. And, as stated, narrative accounts of dreams were collected among graduate students at the University of Jos (from 1987 to 1996) and Kenyatta University (from 1997 to 2008). What one can learn from the sources of data used by Nwoye (2017b) is that AP researchers need to embrace flexibility and selective pluralism or a selective pragmatic philosophy of science to conduct such a transformative study that pools data from different sources with varied time periods. The implications are that (1) primary and secondary data can be used in the same data for triangulation, (2) AP researchers can use accounts of a phenomenon reported by people who have not experienced it as a valid source of data, (3) datasets from different time periods can be analysed together as long as they relate to the same research question, (4) document review can be a source of data, and (5) AP research can use a mix of different sources of data (primary versus secondary, field data versus documents, new data versus old data, etc.) to answer a research question.

On the issue of analysis, much has been written about qualitative analysis to warrant a new discussion in this Element. However, most writings on qualitative analysis have been written through the lens of hegemonic social science (see Smith, 2015). However, there are specific methods, such as discourse analysis, interpretative phenomenological analysis, and grounded theory, that can still be used with a good dose of relational ontology. In practice, many AP researchers tend to use thematic analysis and content analysis as these analytic tools can accommodate different theoretical framing and datasets. The most significant observations that should be noted when analysing interview data are issues of the introjection and ventriloquation that characterise the speech of an African. A good question to ask is whether the themes identified are to be understood as personal accounts or *personalised social accounts* (what every-one knows and believes in a given African community). It is very important for the AP researchers to clarify during interviews as to whether accounts given by research participants are their own thoughts or reflect what others say in the community. When this is not done, the default position will be that the accounts contain community thoughts about the phenomenon being studied. Therefore, qualitative research done in Africa without attempts at distinguishing personal accounts from community thoughts have generalizability power similar to what quantitative methodologists associate with quantitative methodologies. This is one reason qualitative methodology is a preferred approach for conducting AP research. The data you collect, though from a small sample size, tends to reflect an entire community view on a topic if saturation is achieved.

6 Praxis in IPA

To talk about theories and research practices in AP without talking about some applications will create an impression that AP has nothing to do with improving the well-being of Africans. As I have argued already, one of the main reasons for decolonising and indigenising psychology in Africa is to make it more relevant to Africans (Oppong, 2013b, 2014, 2016, 2017, 2019a, 2020b, 2020b, 2022a; also see Dziwornu & Oppong, 2023; Oppong Asante & Oppong, 2012; Oppong et al., 2014). Therefore, a good place to end this Element is to consider a selection of applications of AP, one of which is only being discussed based on its potential usefulness and not on actual use (i.e., *Tiboa* Exploration and Animation Therapy). These selections are only meant to be illustrative.

6.1 Friendship Bench

Developed in Harare, Zimbabwe, in 2006, the Friendship Bench has been running in primary care settings. The Friendship Bench is a task-shifting and task-sharing intervention that trains and deploys lay health workers (grand-mother health providers) to deliver a structured cognitive behaviour therapy (CBT) that relies mainly on problem-solving therapy (PST) (Abas et al., 2016; Chibanda, Mesu et al., 2011; Chibanda, Verhey et al., 2016). The lay health workers are *ambuya utano* (grandmother health providers) who are employed by the City of Harare Health Education Unit for its health promotion. It is delivered by these grandmother health providers on a 'Friendship Bench' (*Chigaro Chekupanamazano*) placed in the clinic grounds for that purpose (Abas et al., 2016; Chibanda, Mesu et al., 2011). They have incorporated indigenous language about mental health into the intervention and deployed the African respect for the elderly in general and grandmothers in particular in the design and delivery of the intervention (see Tsamaase et al., 2020). This is a low-cost approach to scaling access to mental health services that take into account the cultural practices and beliefs of the community. This can be adopted and deployed in other low-income settings. The focus on problem-solving therapy is also consistent with the view that psychoanalytic therapies generally do not work with Africans as they look for material and spiritual solutions to their problems (Oppong, 2017; Oppong et al., 2020). Intervention studies support the usefulness of the *Friendship Bench* in reducing common mental health problems (Chibanda, Mesu et al., 2011; Chibanda, Weiss et al., 2016). For more details about this innovative intervention that respects African cultural values, consult the website at www.friendshipbenchzimbabwe.org/.

6.2 Tales and African Mythology Psychotherapy (Tampsy)

Tampsy stands for Tales and African Mythology Psychotherapy, or Optoa, which (in French), stands for Psychosocial Tool of African Oral Tradition. Tampsy was developed by a Senegalese psychologist, Ismahan Soukeyna Diop, who holds a Ph.D. in clinical psychology and is based at the Department of Psychology, Cheikh Anta Diop University, in Dakar, Senegal. Tampsy is a therapeutic approach that leverages mythology's role as a vehicle of transmission, symbolisation, and elaboration in African oral traditions to support communication about mental health challenges (American Psychological Association [APA], 2021). Accordingly, Tampsy 'has the basic objectives of training and supporting community workers, and above all, contributing to community mental health for the promotion of a more holistic and sustainable management of psychological and psychiatric disorders' (APA, 2021, para. 6). Tampsy can be used by social workers for psychoeducation and clinical or counselling psychologists as a psychotherapy method. Folklores are considered a medium through which to symbolise mental health challenges and connect with clients as the stories are extracted from folk literature with which they are familiar. In therapy sessions, clients are encouraged through storytelling to share examples of their own experiences in order to discuss their potential reaction if they were the character in the story. In this way, the clients identify themselves in the story and choose how to deal with social and personal issues.

This implies that Tampsy works well with clients with existential crises or non-psychotic disorders as it requires a certain level of time and space orientation. Thus, Tampsy provides 'a culturally relevant projective method to apprehend unconscious conflicts' (APA, 2021, para. 10). The central tool in Tampy is storytelling as Africa is endowed with oral traditions. This view is consistent with Nwoye's (2006) adaptation and use of a narrative approach to child and family therapy at Kenyatta University Counselling Centre in Nairobi, Kenya. Both approaches generally resonate with the African oral tradition and remind us of the anthropology-like approach to AP that is needed to deploy cultural materials to promote the well-being of Africans. For more details about this therapeutic intervention, visit the following website: https://tampsy-optoa.com/en/about/.

6.3 *Panga Munthu* Test

The next application I will present here relates to psychological assessment. The use of imported psychological assessment tools in Africa has been heavily criticised as misplaced or dangerous (Oppong, 2015a, 2023c; Oppong et al., 2022). Within a similar context and criticisms, Phuti et al. (2023) have developed and validated a Soft Skills Assessment Scale in Botswana, while Kathuria and Serpell (1998) developed and validated the *Panga Munthu* Test (PMT) (to wit: 'Make a Person' Test) in Zambia. I focus on PMT here as it is a foundational work in psychological testing performed in Africa. PMT presents the child with clay without any model as a guide to copy; in many ways, PMT is similar to the American Draw-a-Person Test (Oppong, 2015a). PMT measures the general cognitive ability of a child relative to his or her peers (Kathuria & Serpell, 1998). To validate PMT, Kathuria and Serpell (1998) collected data from a sample consisting of 3,231 children (males = 1,696 and females = 1,527 with 8 missing information on gender; urban = 1,825 and rural = 1,398) with a mean age of 10.08 years. PMT has a 25-point scoring criteria. The 'person' made by a child is rated from 0 to 1 point for each of the criteria on the 25-point scoring criteria except for the twenty-fourth criterion, which is rated from 0 to 2. PMT shows group effects for grade/class and gender but not place of residence (rural versus urban) and PMT scores correlate highly with age and grade. Test norms are also available to interpret PMT scores (Kathuria & Serpell, 1998). Though not widely used in clinical assessment in Africa, PMT is one of the most culturally appropriate tools to use to assess general cognitive ability or even the neurodevelopment challenges of an African child. It is low cost as it relies on the use of clay, a resource Africa has in abundance. All it requires to administer PMT is a piece of clay and access to the 25-point scoring criteria with the test norms, which are available in Kathuria and Serpell (1998). I therefore encourage educational psychologists, child psychologists, (applied) developmental psychologists, and other interested professionals to use PMT instead of imported tests such as the Draw-a-Person Test, Wechsler Intelligence Scale for Children (WISC), Wechsler Preschool and Primary Scale of Intelligence (WPPSI), McCarthy Scales of Children's Abilities (MASCA), Kaufman Assessment Battery for Children (KABC), or Wide Range Achievement Test (WRAT) or African tests with heavy Western influence such as the Kilifi Developmental Checklist, Kilifi Developmental Inventory, Developmental Milestone Checklist, or Malawi Developmental Assessment Tool. Perhaps we need to update the norms for contemporary times to adjust for the so-called Flynn effect (Flynn, 2009, 2012).

6.4 *Tiboa* Exploration and Animation Therapy (*T*EAT)

As stated earlier, the Strength of *Tiboa* Scale (S*T*S) has the potential to be used for screening clients whose presenting signs and symptoms are related to non-psychotic disorders. This is because the *tiboa* of clients with neuropsychiatric or psychotic disorders or with conditions often characterised by perceptual disturbances (e.g., schizophrenia, dementia, substance misuse, delirium, severe unipolar depression, etc.) may be described as having a 'dead' *tiboa* in the sense that they usually will lack orientation of self to time, place, and people. Such *tiboa*-screening will also assist the mental health professional to determine the extent to which the client has agency (see the discussions on negotiated agency and social intentionality) and willingness to put in the effort to make the desired change in behaviour, thoughts, and emotional expressions. Another potential use of *tiboa* in therapeutic settings involves what we call *Tiboa* Exploration and Animation Therapy (*T*EAT) – an exploration and animation of one's *tiboa* (Oppong et al., 2023). Given that *T*EAT is at the concept development stage, its modalities for therapy are not yet defined. However, *T*EAT has the potential to enable practitioners to explore in a storytelling fashion to identify 'misalignments' in a person's *tiboa* while engaging in activities that can *animate* or give vigour to the *tiboa*, to be desirous of change or to sustain the momentum to change if there is any in the first place (see Nwoye's (2006) narrative approach to therapy and Tampsy). Though *T*EAT may be potentially useful and effective, I have warned that the Akan saying *afutuo nsakyera onipa gye sɛ nsowhɛ* (to wit: challenges change people, not advising) has therapeutic implications (Oppong, 2017; also see Oppong et al., 2023). The implication is that talk therapies (as modulative modalities as opposed to generative) may not always be as successful as behavioural modification-based therapies that involve some changes to the client's social environment. Thus, *T*EAT coupled with some form of flood-ing to expose the person's *tiboa* to situations that trigger the desired changes may be more effective (Oppong et al., 2023). The *T*EAT or a *tiboa*-informed therapy should be understood to not be about the person per se but more about the 'animal' in a person's headspace, with the aim of causing it to change from within (Oppong et al., 2023).

6.5 Culture-Sensitive Childcare Interventions

In some non-Western cultures, the idea of leaving babies to sleep alone is shocking and making them sleep on their backs unnatural. When my friend was struggling to get her infant son to sleep on his back, her Nigerian mother-in-law, who had raised a large family herself and helped in raising dozens of grandchildren, intervened. This baby needs to sleep on his stomach, she insisted, and my friend relented. It worked; my friend's son slept much better on his stomach.

Katherine Merseth King (2023, para. 6)

Director, Early Childhood Development at Research Triangle Institute (RTI) International

Using culturally relevant models to ground early childhood development (ECD) has been reported to promote successful and sustainable ECD intervention programmes in Africa (Oppong, 2015a; Oppong & Strader, 2022; Scheidecker, Boyette et al., 2023b; Scheidecker, Chaudhary et al, 2023a).The current dominant global framework for ECCE is largely an American family model and promotes parenting practices to children and parents around the world, with Africa being no exception (Funk et al., 2023; Oppong, 2015a, 2023c; Scheidecker, Chaudhary et al., 2023a). Again, the assessment tools used in ECD interventions have been criticised for focusing primarily on generating comparable national datasets while sacrificing cultural specificity and relevance. The assessment tools have also been characterised by a problem of excluding children living with developmental delays, while reliance on the use of proxy indicators has been questioned (Draper et al., 2022; Morelli et al., 2018; Oppong, 2023c; Scheidecker et al., 2022, 2021). The under-representation of children and parents from Africa in psychological research, in general (Arnett, 2008; Rad et al., 2018; Thalmayer et al., 2018), and child research, in particular (Draper et al., 2022; Scheidecker et al., 2021; Singh et al., 2023), has been a focus for discussions. When African children are under-represented in child studies, it limits the generalizability of evidence generated to the experiences of African children and parents (Oppong, 2015a, 2019a, 2020a). Similarly, concerns have also been raised about exclusion of some disciplines (e.g., cultural anthropology, sociology of childhood, cultural psychology, etc.), methodologies (i.e., qualitative approaches), and evidence types (e.g., ethnographic scientific evidence) from knowledge production, programme design, policy influence, funding, and visibility (Draper et al., 2022; King, 2023; Oppong, 2023c; Scheidecker, Chaudhary et al, 2023a). There have also been calls for recognition of indigenous theories of children's development, including cultural practices to prepare children for membership of their communities (Dar & Lyså, 2022; Funk et al., 2023; Oppong, 2015a, 2022a ; Oppong & Strader, 2022; Pence et al., 2023; Tsamaase et al., 2020).

Despite all these issues, the desire of most global ECD practitioners and researchers (who are often from Western societies) 'to improve child well-being at scale impels' them 'to pursue uniform approaches; that is, the one package that can be used everywhere to good effect. International organisations promote "signature programs" – helped along by catchy names and sleek marketing – that apply universal guidance in broadly diverse contexts' (King, 2023, para. 12). These concerns have led many Africa-based child developmental psychologists and ECD researchers, in the spirit of AP, to challenge the Western orthodoxy about ECD research in Africa (Apolot et al., 2020; Ejuu, 2015; Oppong, 2015a, 2023c; Pence et al., 2023). As a result, some have gone ahead to develop guidelines and recommendations for culturally appropriate ECD interventions for implementation (Ejuu, 2019; Ejuu, Apolot et al., 2022; Ejuu & Opiyo, 2022; Ejuu, Locoro et al., 2022; Oppong, 2022c; Oppong & Strader, 2022). Currently, there exists a practical resource for enhancing cultural relevance of ECD interventions in Africa through culture-sensitive planning, design, implementation, and evaluation (Oppong & Strader, 2022); an equally good resource to guide the design of culturally relevant ECD interventions by Pence et al. (2023); and other attempts at designing and implementing culturally relevant ECD interventions in East and Southern Africa, including inclusive home-based early childhood education (Ejuu, 2019; Ejuu, Locoro et al., 2022; Ejuu & Opiyo, 2022; Tafirenyika et al., 2023). These ECD interventions are designed to take advantage of indigenous knowledge about child-rearing practices and community support systems that exist in those communities. For instance, these ECD interventions make use of community cultural assets such as indigenous games, songs, puzzles, stories, and others to support early learning of young children in those communities, such as the inclusive child-to-child learning approach and inclusive home-based early learning projects in Uganda (Nafungo & Ejuu, 2022; Nafungo et al., 2022). The Child-to-Child Project in Uganda, Ethiopia, and Malawi – a Knowledge Innovation Exchange (KIX) projected funded by the Global Partnership for Education and International Development Research Centre – deserves a special mention here (GPE-KIX, 2024). The Child-to-Child Project has compiled 200 indigenous games and songs in Uganda to develop an activity pack for 3-to-8-year-olds as well as a caregiver guide (GPE-KIX, 2024). Similarly, the same project has compiled about fifty indigenous games and songs in Ethiopia in the Amharic language (an official language in Ethiopia) for use (GPE-KIX, 2024). In addition to compiling indigenous resources for education, the Child-to-Child Project also takes advantage of the fact that early learning in Africa is partly promoted through peer-to-peer learning in multi-age play groups among young children (GPE-KIX, 2024; Scheidecker et al., 2023b); thus, it employs a naturally occurring cultural strategy in African communities to promote early learning or early childhood education. Another example is the Insaka integrated early childhood development (ECD) programme in the Katete and Petauke districts of Zambia (UNICEF, 2021). This programme leverages African communal gathering points (i.e., the village square) and communal support to deliver ECD initiatives. Though cast in the dominant global ECD paradigm, it still uses a key cultural value as a platform for intervention implementation. This example is cited to illustrate the usefulness of African cultural values to project implementation.

7 Epilogue

I will start the conclusion by attempting to set some records straight as they relate to my legitimate authority to theorise for AP and be a key contributor to AP. I received my master's-level training in industrial and organisational psychology and obtained a Ph.D. in general psychology, doing my doctoral research in cultural ergonomics. However, most of the AP contributors have come from subfields of psychology such as clinical psychology, counselling psychology, developmental psychology, and community psychology. For instance, Jiyane (2022), in her qualitative study on how AP scholars conceptualise Black psychological empowerment, interviewed fourteen AP scholars, of whom twelve are within the healthcare subfields of psychology (ten clinical and two counselling psychologists), along with one research psychologist and one industrial and organisational psychologist. I am not sure of the ethics of revealing personal identification information about research participants, but if I may, I will use the right to privacy and confidentiality to imply the right to also agree to be named. Therefore, acting in that ethical understanding, I wish to state that I was the industrial and organisational psychologist participant in that study (noting that I am by primary training in psychology). This goes to show the paucity of other subfields of psychology in AP, as if AP belongs to only the healthcare subfields. In a similar vein, Tedd Judd, a cross-cultural neuropsychologist, described my work on the African theory of intelligence as 'great, and groundbreaking!' but argued that 'This is exactly the kind of questioning of fundamental assumptions that we have been hoping for from a real cultural neuropsychology [sic], even though he comes from I/O psychology' (Tedd Judd, personal communication, December 30, 2020). This is critical for me to clarify a few issues. In many ways, I feel like a loner in AP and in other areas like history and theory of psychology and ECD research. I came to AP for the many reasons I have already outlined in this Element (see 1.6 Significance of Establishing IPA). I contend that it is only when the fundamentals of AP are built that we can fully apply it to other sectors of the economy or aspects of our life in Africa. However, I also believe that the involvement of many Africa-based psychologists with different subfield interests will go a long way to help create concepts, theories, and applications in other areas of psychology.

The other record that needs to be set straight relates to my actual or imagined relation to Kwame Gyekye (1939–2019). I am related to Kwame Gyekye through my father, as Gyekye was his grandson in the extended family system (Gyekye was older than my father at the time of his passing; may his soul rest in perfect peace; let's observe a minute of silence for a fallen hero of African philosophy). I never met him as a student at the University of Ghana, Legon, though, as I later understood, he was still at the university. I am bringing this up so that historians and psychologists will not have to debate about it ever. In many ways, I see my work as a sort of intellectual continuity of a legacy in the psychology–philosophy nexus.

To conclude, I would like to repeat some of my previous conclusions presented elsewhere here (Oppong, 2022a). This is because this Element is true to the core arguments contained in Oppong (2022a). Thus, I conclude that (1) AP has come to stay, but it requires current teachers of psychology in Africa to train students in AP. I wish to call for a consideration to mount AP modules in psychology departments across Africa; (2) grounding oneself in AP requires self-training, for now, in history of psychology, philosophy of (social) science, the science of science, African philosophy, African cultural anthropology, African sociolinguistics, and sociology of knowledge; (3) a boundaryless orientation to the study of human nature that takes useful ideas from evidence is emerging in cognate disciplines considering the fact that there are four distinct strands of AP currently; (4) AP has relevance for understanding Africans as well as policy work in Africa, thus contributing to the growth and development of Africa; and (5) AP can and should contribute to global psychology so that students of humanity can benefit from diverse perspectives and views about human nature, thus supporting the cultivation of cultural competence in both Africa-based psychologists and non-Africa-based psychologists.

On the first conclusion that AP has come to stay, there are already signs of departments of psychology based outside of Africa showing interest in teaching AP or at least having a concentration on African and Caribbean mental health (a Google search will reveal many). When asked to count an AP module, most struggle to know where to start. I will provide the following recommendations: (1) this very Element is a good source to use to develop content for teaching an AP module; (2) you may use this Element together with Nwoye's (2022) *African Psychology: The Emergence of a Tradition*; and 3) you can also use other books in the Pan-African Psychologies book series (see https://link .springer.com/series/15830/books). I will also provide a sample course outline as a guide (see Table 4). There is also a need to decide as to whether AP should be developed into a minor/part qualification with a defined curriculum. I support such a move to teach AP as a minor/part qualification until we can develop AP into a full-blown single major qualification or, at least, create a graduate-level specialisation in psychology in Africa and elsewhere.

Table 4 Content extracted from the African Psychology Module developed at Eswatini Medical Christian University

Course Description: This module ... is designed to introduce students to the wealth of ideas, philosophies, knowledge systems, and frameworks emanating from Africa. This epistemological and methodological shift is done with the intent of social justice, that is, to restore justice and dignity to Africans (sub-Saharan Africa) through decolonisation and to affirm the idea that African experiences, realities, and ideas are important, matter, and are valid in the field of psychology. This module will examine a variety of topical areas in psychology from diverse African cultural perspectives and offer avenues for reflection on the interaction between African psychology and globalisation.

Objectives: At the successful completion of this module, students will be able to:
(1) Critically, logically, and systematically engage with multiple African psychology/epistemology theories in different contexts.
(2) Achieve an understanding of the African philosophical concept of Ubuntu and its ideas of the self in relation to self, community, wholeness, and collective consciousness.
(3) Understand the characteristics of Africa's indigenous knowledge.
(4) Conceptualise, analyse, and formulate African psychological matters using indigenous theorisations, worldviews, and conceptions in a culturally nuanced manner.

(5) Contrast and compare African and Western theories of psychology and situate them within their historical–cultural contexts.
(6) Demonstrate an understanding of the role of spirituality in the lives of indigenous people.
(7) Understand African explanatory models of illness and well-being.
(8) Reflect on the intersection of African psychology with globalisation.

Schedule of Topics

(1) **Introduction to African Psychology and Definition of Key Concepts** (Is there African Psychology? Philosophy; Epistemology; Ontology; Culture; Scope; and Questions about African Psychology)
(2) **Justification for Africa Psychology** (Link between Psychology and Colonialism in Africa; Quest for Relevance)
(3) **Methods of Knowing** (African Ways of Knowing and Pedagogy; Characteristics of African Indigenous Knowledge; Afrocentric Methodology; Proverbs as Method of Knowledge Production)
(4) **Development and Socialisation** (in the context)
(5) **Self, Personhood, and Community in African Traditional Thoughts** (Ubuntu Philosophy; Contrasts between African Conception of the Person and Western Conception of the Person; Conceptualising Personhood, Agency, and Morality for African Psychology)
(6) **Mental Health and Illness** (Comparison of Western and African Paradigms on Mental Health & Illness; Africentric Paradigm to Clinical Diagnosis and Treatment; Experience and Meaning of Recovery for an African Population)
(7) **Globalisation and the Future of African Culture** (Globalisation and Culture; Globalisation and the African Experience; Strategies for Stemming the Tide of Cultural; Atrophy of African Culture)
(8) **Indigenisation of Psychology** (The Concept of Decolonisation/ Indigenisation and Practical Implementation; Challenges of Indigenisation; Indigenising Knowledge for Development)
(9) **Philosophy of Science and Research Methodology in African Psychology**

Assigned Readings:

[8] Adair, J. G. (1999). Indigenisation of psychology: The concept and its practical implementation.*Applied Psychology*, *48*(4), 403–18. https://doi.org/10.1111/j.1464–0597.1999.tb00062.x

[5] Adjei, S. B. (2019). Conceptualising personhood, agency, and morality for African psychology.*Theory & Psychology*, *29*(4), 484–505. https://doi.org/10.1177/0959354319857473

[8] Allwood, C. M. (2018).*The nature and challenges of indigenous psychologies*. Cambridge University Press.

[6] Asare, M., & Danquah, S. A. (2017). The African belief system and the patient's choice of treatment from existing health models: The case of Ghana.*Acta Psychopathologica*, *3*(4), 49. https://doi.org/ 10.4172/2469–6676.100121

[6] Baloyi, L., & Ramose, M.B. (2016). Psychology and psychotherapy redefined from the viewpoint of the African experience (Special Edition).*Alternation*, *18*, 12–35. https://journals.ukzn.ac.za/index .php/soa/article/view/1352

[2] Bandawe, C. (2005). Psychology brewed in an African pot: Indigenous philosophies and the quest for relevance.*Higher Education Policy*, *18*, 289–300. https://eric.ed.gov/?id=EJ745010

[9] Chilisa, B. (2019).*Indigenous research methodologies* (2nd ed.). Sage.

[2] Holdstock, T. L. (1981). Psychology in South Africa belongs to the colonial era: Arrogance or ignorance?*South African Journal of Psychology*, *11*(4), 123–9. https://citeseerx.ist.psu.edu/viewdoc/ download?doi=10.1.1.1017.9005&rep=rep1&type=pdf

[2] Long, W. (2013). Rethinking 'relevance': South African psychology in context.*History of Psychology*, *16*(1), 19–35. https://doi.org/ 10.1037/a0029675

[5] Menkiti, I. A. (1984). Person and community in African traditional thought. In R. A. Wright (Ed.),*African philosophy: An introduction* (3rd ed., pp. 171–81). University Press of America.

[1,2 & 3] Mubangizi, O. (n.d.). Wisdom of the elders: African proverbs as a methodology for knowledge production in Africa. www.academia.edu/ 25728676/African_Proverbs_A_Method_of_Knowledge_ Production_in_Africa

[4] Mwamwenda, T. (1996).*Educational psychology: An African perspective* (2nd ed). Heinemann Publishers.

[3] Ngara, C. (2007). African ways of knowing and pedagogy revisited.*Journal of Contemporary Issues in Education*, *2*(2), 7–21. https://doi.org/10.20355/C5301M

[6] Ngubane, S. N., McAndrew, S., & Collier, E. (2019). The experiences and meanings of recovery for Swazi women living with 'schizophrenia'.*Journal of Psychiatric and Mental Health Nursing*, *26*(5–6), 153–62. https://doi.org/10.1111/jpm.12520

[6] Nwoye, A. (2015). African psychology and the Africentric paradigm to clinical diagnosis and treatment.*South African Journal of Psychology*, *45*(3), 305–17. https://doi.org/10.1177/00812463 15570960.

[9] Nwoye, A. (2022).*African psychology: The emergence of a tradition*. Oxford University Press. https://doi.org/10.1093/oso/9780190932497.001.0001

[7] Obioha, P. U. (2010). Globalization and the future of African culture.*Philosophical Papers and Reviews*, *2*(1), 1–8. https://doi.org/10.5897/PPR.9000005

[8] Oppong, S. (2013). Indigenizing knowledge for development: Epistemological and pedagogical approaches.*Africanus*, *43*(2), 34–50. https://doi.org/10.25159/0304–615X/2300

[9] Oppong, S. (2014). A critique of the philosophical underpinnings of mainstream social science research.*Academicus*, *5*(10), 242–54. https://doi.org/10.7336/academicus.2014.10.17

[2&8] Oppong, S. (2019). Overcoming obstacles to a truly global psychological theory, research, and praxis in Africa.*Journal of Psychology in Africa*, *29*(4), 292–300. https://doi.org/10.1080/14330237.2019.1647497

[1] Oppong, S. (2022). Indigenous psychology in Africa: Centrality of culture, misunderstandings, and global positioning.*Theory & Psychology*, *32*(6), 953–73. https://doi.org/10.1177/095935432 21097334

[9] Oppong, S. (2022). On mainstreaming philosophy of science in psychology through 'psychological theoretics'.*Annals of Psychology*, *XXV* (1), 27–45. https://doi.org/10.18290/rpsych2022.0002

[4] Oppong, S. (2023). Promoting global ECD top-down and bottom-up. *Ethos*. https://doi.org/10.1111/etho.12393

[8] Oppong, S. (2023). Epistemological allyship.*Psychology and Developing Societies*, *35*(1), 69–86. https://doi.org/10.1177/0971333 6231152301

[5] Oppong, S. (2023). An indigenous representation of personhood for citizenship behaviours. In J. Osafo & C. S. Akotia (Eds.), *Personhood, community and the human condition: Reflections and applications in the African experience* (pp. 27–47). Ayebia Clarke Publishing Limited.

[2, 5 & 8] Oppong, S., Ajei, M. O., & Majeed, H. M. (2023). Nurturing the nexus between African philosophy and African psychology.*The American Philosophical Association Studies*, *23*(1), 141–6. https://cdn.ymaws.com/www.apaonline.org/resource/collection/C29D5481–4D0D–4E09–81F3–8C5DC2148822/APAStudiesFall2023.pdf.

[3] Owusu-Ansah, F. E., & Mji, G. (2013). African indigenous knowledge and research. *African Journal of Disability*, *2*(1), 1–5. http://doi.org/10.4102/ajod.v2i1.30

[2 & 8] Pheko, M. M. (2017). Decolonising and indigenising the psychology curriculum: Reflections and key lessons from the 2017 Pan-African Psychology Union (Papu 2017) Conference.*Lonaka Journal of Teaching & Learning*, *8* (1), 105–11. https://journals.ub.bw/index.php/jolt/article/view/1092

[8] Pillay, S. R. (2017). Cracking the fortress: can we really decolonize psychology?*South African Journal of Psychology*, *47*(2), 135–40. https://doi.org/10.1177/0081246317698059.

[1] Ratele, K. (2017). Six theses on African psychology for the world. *Psychology in Society*, *54*, 1–9. http://doi.org/10.17159/2309–8708/2017/n54a1

[1 & 2] Ratele, K. (2017). Frequently asked questions about African psychology.*South African Journal of Psychology*, *47*(3), 273–9. https://doi.org/10.1177/0081246317703249.

[8] Ratele, K., Cornell, J., Dlamini, S., Helman, R., Malherbe, N., & Titi, N. (2018). Some basic questions about (a) decolonizing Africa (n)-centred psychology considered. *South African Journal of Psychology*, *48*(3), 331–42. https://doi.org/10.1177/0081246318790444

Source: Adapted from Oppong (2022a, pp. 972–3).

Finally, AP should be seen as a legitimate science of African human experience that should expand to include applications in different spheres of life in an African community. One way to achieve this is to pursue interdisciplinarity in AP and take from cognate fields whatever is useful to provide new insight. I also challenge Africa-based psychologists to take up the quest to develop a psychology that is authentically about understanding Africans to inform policies to improve their well-being. As there is nothing more useful than a good theory (Oppong, 2022b), Africa-based psychologists should seek to contribute in theory development more often, as they have contributed more in empirical research. This is not to say Africa-based psychologists should abandon their current work in empirical studies. Rather, I suggest that the empirical work should contribute to building culturally relevant theories to account for the human experience of the African. However, I will join Mpofu (2002) in cautioning AP researchers and practitioners not to have a romantic view of African culture nor to fail to understand that there are both cultural differences and similarities. Though a principal focus on AP is to explore those cultural differences to develop appropriate explanatory systems for the African experience, there is equally a need to employ the cultural similarities to develop theories that apply to all humans regardless of one's culture. AP should, therefore, not be seen to be engaging in meaningless rejection of good ideas from other disciplines and cultural settings.

References

Abas, M., Bowers, T., Manda, E., et al. (2016). 'Opening up the mind': Problem-solving therapy delivered by female lay health workers to improve access to evidence-based care for depression and other common mental disorders through the Friendship Bench Project in Zimbabwe. *International Journal of Mental Health Systems, 10*, 39. https://doi.org/10.1186/s13033-016-0071-9.

Adjei, S. B. (2017). Entrapment of victims of spousal abuse in Ghana: A discursive analysis of family identity and agency of battered women. *Journal of Interpersonal Violence, 32*(5), 730–54. https://doi.org/10.1177/0886260515586375.

Adjei, S. B. (2018). The social intentionality of battered women's agency in Ghana. *Psychology and Developing Societies, 30*(1), 1–18. https://doi.org/10.1177/0971333617747320.

African Commission on Human and Peoples' Rights (ACHPR) and International Work Group for Indigenous Affairs (IWGIA). (2005). *Report of the African Commission's working group on indigenous populations/communities.* www.iwgia.org/images/publications/African_Commission_book.pdf.

African Development Bank Group. (2016). African Development Bank Group's development and Indigenous Peoples in Africa. *Safeguards And Sustainability Series, 2*(2), 1–29. www.afdb.org/fileadmin/uploads/afdb/Documents/Publications/Development_and_Indigenous_Peoples_in_Africa__En__-_v3_.pdf.

Agyekum, K. (2018). *Akan body parts expressions: Cognitive semantics and pragmatic approach.* Adwinsa Publications (Gh) Ltd.

Agyekum, K. (2020). Akan cultural concepts and expressions for 'stress', 'distress', 'sorrow', and 'depression'. *Nordic Journal of African Studies, 29* (3), 21. https://doi.org/10.53228/njas.v29i3.546.

Ahuma, S. R. B. A. (1905). *Memoirs of West African celebrities: Europe, & c., 1700–1850, with special references to the Gold Coast.* D. Marples.

Ajei, M., & Myles, N. O. (2019). Personhood, autonomy, and informed consent. In Y. A. Frimpong-Mansoh & C. A. Atuire (Eds.), *Bioethics in Africa: Theories and praxis* (pp. 77–94). Vernon Press.

Allwood, C. M. (2018). *The nature and challenges of indigenous psychologies.* Cambridge University Press.

Allwood, C. M. (2019). Comment: Future prospects for indigenous psychologies. *Journal of Theoretical and Philosophical Psychology, 39*(2), 90–7. http://doi.org/10.1037/teo0000108.

American Psychological Association. (2021, February 18). TAMPSY: Tales and African mythology psychotherapy. *Global Insights Newsletter.* www .apa.org/international/global-insights/african-mythology-psychotherapy.

Apolot, J. M., Ejuu, G., & Lubaale, G. (2020). Pursuing quality education in Karamoja: An analysis of the caregivers' quality indicators from a community perspective for sustainable early childhood education programmes. *American Journal of Education and Practice, 4*(1), 72–88. https://doi.org/10.47672/ajep.574.

Appiah, P., Appiah, A., & Agyeman-Duah, I. (2007). *Bu Me Bɛ: Proverbs of the Akans* (2nd ed.). Ayebia Clarke Publishing.

Appiah, A., Fadiji, A. W., Wissing, M. P., & Schutte, L. (2021). Participants' experiences and impressions of a group-based positive psychology intervention programme for rural adults in Ghana. *International Journal of Qualitative Studies on Health and Well-Being, 16*(1), 1891760. https://doi .org/10.1080/17482631.2021.1891760.

Arnett, J. J. (2008). The neglected 95%: Why American psychology needs to become less American. *The American Psychologist, 63*(7), 602–14. https:// doi.org/10.1037/0003066X.63.7.602.

Asante, S. K. B. (2011). *Setting straight the records of Ghana's recent political past.* DigiBooks Ghana Ltd.

Asare, M., & Danquah, S. A. (2017). The African belief system and the patient's choice of treatment from existing health models: The case of Ghana. *Acta Psychopathologica, 3*(4), 1–4. www.primescholars.com/articles/the-african-belief-system-and-the-patients-choice-of-treatment-from-existing-health-modelsthe-case-of-ghana.pdf.

Azibo, D. (2014). The Azibo Nosology II: Epexegesis and 25th anniversary update: 55 culture-focused mental disorders suffered by African descent people. *The Journal of Pan African Studies, 7*(5), 32–145. http://jpanafri can.org/docs/vol7no5/4-Nov-Azibo-Noso.pdf.

Bandura, A. (2018). Toward a psychology of human agency: Pathways and reflections. *Perspectives on Psychological Science, 13*(2), 130–6. https://doi .org/10.1177/1745691617699280.

Brown, N., McIlwraith, T., & de González, L. T. (2020). *Perspectives: An open introduction to cultural anthropology.* American Anthropological Association.

Bruck, J. N. (2020). Long-term memory. In J. Vonk & T. Shackelford (Eds.), *Encyclopedia of animal cognition and behavior* (pp. 1–5). Springer. https:// doi.org/10.1007/978-3-319-47829-6_783-1.

Chibanda, D., Mesu, P., Kajawu, L., et al (2011). Problem-solving therapy for depression and common mental disorders in Zimbabwe: Piloting a task-shifting primary mental health care intervention in a population with a high prevalence of people living with HIV. *BMC Public Health*, *11*, 828. https://doi.org/10.1186/1471-2458-11-828.

Chibanda, D., Verhey, R., Munetsi, E., et al. (2016). Using a theory driven approach to develop and evaluate a complex mental health intervention: The friendship bench project in Zimbabwe. *International Journal of Mental Health Systems*, *10*(16). https://doi.org/10.1186/s13033-016-0050-1.

Chibanda, D., Weiss, H. A., Verhey, R., et al. (2016). Effect of a primary care-based psychological intervention on symptoms of common mental disorders in Zimbabwe: A randomized clinical trial. *JAMA*, *316*(24), 2618–26. https://doi.org/10.1001/jama.2016.19102.

Chilisa, B. (2019). *Indigenous research methodologies* (2nd ed.). Sage.

Christaller, J. G. (1879). *Twi mmebusεm, mpensã-ahansĩa mmoaano: A collection of three thousand and six hundred Tshi proverbs, in use among the Negroes of the Gold Coast speaking the Asante and Fante language, collected, together with their variations, and alphabetically arranged.* Evangelische Missionsgesellschaft.

Dar, A., & Lyså, I. M. (2022). Southern theories and decolonial childhood studies. *Childhood*, *29*(3), 255–75. https://doi.org/10.1177/09075682221111690.

Davis, P. J. (2000). Anthropology and African philosophy: A review essay. *The CLR James Journal*, *7*(1), 151–63. www.jstor.org/stable/26759427.

Draper, C. E., Barnett, L. M., Cook, C. J., et al. (2022). Publishing child development research from around the world: An unfair playing field resulting in most of the world's child population under-represented in research. *Infant and Child Development*, *32*(6), e2375. https://doi.org/10.1002/icd.2375.

Dziwornu, E., & Oppong, S. (2023). Opportunities for growing psychology due to the COVID-19 pandemic in a non-Western context: the case of Ghana in West Africa. *Ghana Social Science Journal*, *20*(1), 58–70. https://journals.ug.edu.gh/index.php/gssj/article/view/2278.

Dzokoto, V. A. (2020). Adwenhoasem: An Akan theory of mind. *Journal of the Royal Anthropological Institute*, *26*(S1), 77–94. https://doi.org/10.1111/1467-9655.13242.

Dzokoto, V. A., Osei-Tutu, A., Kyei, J. J., et al. (2018). Emotion norms, display rules, and regulation in the Akan Society of Ghana: An exploration using proverbs. *Frontiers in Psychology*, *9*, 1916. https://doi.org/10.3389/fpsyg.2018.01916.

Ejuu, G. (2015). Is this early childhood development ours? Deciphering what African parents want their children to learn in early childhood development. *Teachers' Work*, *12*(1), 30–44. https://doi.org/10.24135/teacherswork.v12i1.44.

Ejuu, G. (2019). African indigenous games: Using Bame Nsamenang's Africentric thoughts to reflect on our heritage, pedagogy, and practice in a global village. *Journal of Psychology in Africa, 29*(4), 319–27. https://doi .org/10.1080/14330237.2019.1647496.

Ejuu, G., Apolot, J. M., & Serpell, R. (2022). Early childhood education quality indicators: Exploring the landscape of an African community perspective. *Global Studies of Childhood, 12*(2), 170–80. https://doi.org/10.1177/ 2043610619832898.

Ejuu, G., & Opiyo, R. A. (2022). Nurturing Ubuntu, the African form of human flourishing through inclusive home based early childhood education. *Frontiers in Education, 7*, 838770. https://doi.org/10.3389/feduc.2022 .838770.

Ejuu, G., Locoro, V., Miria, N., et al. (2022). Community's knowledge, attitude and practices towards inclusive home based early childhood education in Uganda: Lessons for scaling deep. S*outh African Journal of Childhood Education, 12*(1), 1–7. https://doi.org/10.4102/sajce.v12i1.1117.

Flew, A. (Ed.). (1962). *David Hume: On human nature and the understanding.* Macmillan.

Flynn, J. R. (2009). *What is intelligence? Beyond the Flynn effect.* Cambridge University Press. https://doi.org/10.1017/CBO9780511605253.

Flynn J. R. (2012). *Are we getting smarter? Rising IQ in the twenty-first century.* Cambridge University Press. https://doi.org/10.1017/CBO9781139235679.

Funk, L., Scheidecker, G., Chapin, B. L., et al. (2023). *Feeding, bonding, and the formation of social relationships: Ethnographic challenges to attachment theory and early childhood interventions.* Cambridge University Press. https://doi.org/10.1017/9781009306300.

Gavi, J. K., Akotia, C. S., Osafo, J., et al. (2022). Conceptions of personhood in Ghana: An emic perspective. *Ghana Social Sciences Journal, 19*(1), 16–31. https://journals.ug.edu.gh/index.php/gssj/article/view/1905/1094.

GPE-KIX. (2024). Inclusive child to child learning approach: Scaling up inclusive play based learning for smooth transition from pre-priary to primary school. Retrieved March 16, 2024 from: www.gpekix.org/project/inclusive-child-child-learning-approach-scaling-inclusive-play-based-learning-smooth.

Greenwood, E. (1976). Attributes of a profession. In N. Gilbert & H. Specht (Eds.), *Emergence of social welfare and social work* (pp. 302–18.). Peacock Publishers.

Grigorenko, E. L., Geissler, P. W., Prince, R., et al. (2001). The organisation of Luo conceptions of intelligence: A study of implicit theories in a Kenyan village. *International Journal of Behavioral Development, 25*(4), 367–78. https://doi.org/10.1080/01650250042000348.

Gyekye, K. (1978). The Akan concept of person. *International Philosophical Quarterly, 18*(3), 277–87. https://doi.org/10.5840/ipq197818329.

Gyekye, K. (2003). *African cultural values: An introduction.* Sankofa Publishing Company.

Hambrick, D. C., & Chen, M.-J. (2008). New academic fields as admittance-seeking social movements: The case of strategic management. *The Academy of Management Review, 33*(1), 32–54. www.jstor.org/stable/20159375.

Hapunda, G. (2022). Caregiving roles of female guardians, older siblings, and time spent on child activities. *Family Relations, 72*(4), 1–12. https://doi.org/10.1111/fare.12762.

Hergenhahn, B. R. (2009). *An introduction to the history of psychology.* Cengage Learning.

Jahoda, G. (2016). Seventy years of social psychology: A cultural and personal critique. *Journal of Social and Political Psychology, 4*(1), 364–80. https://doi.org/10.5964/jspp.v4i1.621.

Janz, B. (2007). African philosophy. In C. Boundas (Ed.), *Companion to 20th century Philosophy* (pp. 689–701). Edinburgh University Press.

Jiyane, M. S. (2022). *How Africa(n)-centred psychology scholars conceptualise Black psychological empowerment* [Unpublished doctoral thesis]. University of Johannesburg.

Johnson, J. (2018). *Anthropology and the study of Africa.* In *Oxford research encyclopedia of African History.* Oxford University Press. https://doi.org/10.1093/acrefore/9780190277734.013.179.

Jovanović, G. (2005). Theoretical challenges of internationalizing psychological knowledge. In A. Gülerce, A. Hofmeister, I. Staeuble, G. Saunders, & J. Kaye (Eds.), *Contemporary theorizing in psychology: Global perspectives* (pp. 78–87). Captus Press.

Jukes, M. C. H., Sitabkhan, Y., and Tibenda, J. J. (2021b). *Adapting pedagogy to cultural context.* RTI Press Publication No. OP-0070-2109. RTI Press. https://doi.org/10.3768/rtipress.2021.op.0070.2109.

Kathuria, R., & Serpell, R. (1998). Standardization of the Panga Munthu Test: A nonverbal cognitive test developed in Zambia. *Journal of Negro Education, 67*, 228–41. https://doi.org/10.2307/2668192.

Keller, H. (2016). Psychological autonomy and hierarchical relatedness as organizers of developmental pathways. *Philosophical Transactions of the Royal Society of London, Series B, Biological Sciences, 371*(1686), 20150070. https://doi.org/10.1098/rstb.2015.0070.

Ketsitlile, L. (2013). An integrative review on the San of Botswana's Indigenous literacy and formal schooling education. *The Australian Journal of Indigenous Education, 41*(2), 218–28. https://doi.org/10.1017/jie.2012.21.

King, K. M. (2023, July 25). *Becoming a parent is changing how I approach early childhood development programming.* www.rti.org/insights/how-to-approach-early-childhood-development-programming.

Kluckhohn, C., & Kelly, W. H. (1945). The concept of culture. In R. Linton (Ed.), *The science of man in the world crisis* (pp. 78–105). Columbia University Press.

Laher, S., & Hassem, T. (2020). Doing systematic reviews in psychology. *South African Journal of Psychology, 50*(4), 450–68. https://doi.org/10.1177/0081246320956417.

Lamont, M. (2019). How to publish, but most importantly, why. *Sociologica, 13* (1), 33–5. https://doi.org/10.6092/issn.1971-8853/9384.

Louw, D. A., & Louw, A. E. (2014). *Child and adolescent development* (2nd ed.). Psychology Publications.

Lowie, R. H. (1953). Ethnography, cultural and social anthropology. *American Anthropologist, 55*(4), 527–34. https://escholarship.org/uc/item/9t13v9kz.

Mafela, L. (2014). Education and perceptions of 'Other': Colonial education of Batswana and formal education of Indigenous San in Botswana. *AlterNative: An International Journal of Indigenous Peoples, 10*(1), 45–57. https://doi .org/10.1177/117718011401000105.

Mazrui, A. A. (2005). Pan-Africanism and the intellectuals: Rise, decline, and revival. In T. Mkandawire (Ed.), *African intellectuals: Rethinking politics, language, gender, and development* (pp. 56–77). Zed Books.

Mbiti, J. S. (1969). *African religions and philosophy.* East African Educational Publisher.

Merriam-Webster. (n.d.). *Orientation.* In Merriam-Webster.com Dictionary. Retrieved March 8, 2023, from www.merriam-webster.com/dictionary/orientation.

Mignolo, W. D. (2009). Epistemic disobedience, independent thought and decolonial freedom. *Theory, Culture and Society, 26*(7–8), 159–81. https://doi.org/10.1177/0263276409349275.

Mkhize, N. (2013). Psychology: An African perspective. In D. Hook, N. Mkhize, P. Kiguwa, & A. Collins (Eds.), *Critical psychology* (pp. 24–52). Juta and Company.

Molosiwa, A. A., & Galeforolwe, D. (2018). Child rearing practices of the San communities in Botswana: Potential lessons for educators. *AlterNative: An International Journal of Indigenous Peoples, 14*(2) 130–7. https://doi.org/10.1177/1177180118772601.

Morelli, G., Quinn, N., Chaudhary, N., et al. (2018). Ethical challenges of parenting interventions in low-to middle-income countries. *Journal of Cross-Cultural Psychology, 49*(1), 5–24.

Mpofu, E. (2002). Psychology in sub-Saharan Africa: Challenges, prospects and promises. *International Journal of Psychology, 37*(3), 179–86. https://doi.org/10.1080/00207590244000061.

Nafungo, J., & Ejuu, G. (2022, December 1). *Early learning unlocks potential for children with disabilities and developmental delays*. Retrieved August 8, 2023 from www.gpekix.org/blog/early-learning-unlocks-potential-children-disabilities-and-developmental-delays.

Nafungo, J., Wind, T., Jamtsho, S., et al. (2022, March 31). '*Playful beginnings': New KIX research collaborations for better early learning*. Retrieved August 8, 2023 from www.gpekix.org/blog/playful-beginnings-new-kix-research-collaborations-better-early-learning.

Naidoo, A. V. (1996). Challenging the hegemony of Eurocentric psychology. *Journal of Community and Health Sciences, 2*(2), 9–16.

Nanda, S., & Warms, R. L. (2012). *Culture counts: A concise introduction to cultural anthropology* (2nd ed.). Wadsworth.

Nkwi, P. N. (2015). Introduction: The anthropology of Africa: Challenges for the 21st century. In P. N. Nkwi (Ed.), *The anthropology of Africa: Challenges for the 21st century* (pp. ix–xiv). Langaa RPCIG. https://doi.org/10.2307/j.ctvh9vxg1.3.

Noyau, C., and Gbeto, K.-S. (2004). *Les conceptions de l'intelligence dans la culture éwé: analyse sémantique des expressions du domaine cognitif* [Conceptions of intelligence in Ewe culture: Semantic analysis of expressions in the cognitive domain]. Actes du Congrès de l'ARIC (Association pour la Recherche InterCulturelle) [Proceedings of the Congress of the ARIC (Association for InterCultural Research)], Université d'Amiens, Amiens, France, 30 June–4 July 2003. Actes en ligne: www.unifr.ch/ipg/sitecrt/ARIC/XeCongres/communication.html.

Nsamenang, A. B. (1992). *Human development in a cultural context: A third world perspective*. Sage Publications.

Nsamenang, A. B. (2006). Human ontogenesis: An indigenous African view on development and intelligence. *International Journal of Psychology, 41*(4), 293–7. https://doi.org/10.1080/00207590544000077.

Nwoye, A. (2006). A narrative approach to child and family therapy in Africa. *Contemporary Family Therapy: An International Journal, 28*(1), 1–23. https://doi.org/10.1007/s10591-006-9691-6.

Nwoye, A. (2014). African psychology, critical trends. In T. Teo (Ed.), *Encyclopedia of critical psychology* (pp. 57–65). Springer. https://doi.org/10.1007/978-1-4614-5583-7_483.

Nwoye, A. (2015a). What is African psychology the psychology of? *Theory & Psychology, 25*(1), 96–116. https://doi.org/10.1177/0959354314565116.

Nwoye, A. (2015b). African psychology and the Africentric paradigm to clinical diagnosis and treatment. *South African Journal of Psychology, 45* (3), 305–17. https://doi.org/10.1177/0081246315570960.

Nwoye, A. (2017a). An Africentric theory of human personhood. *Psychology in Society (PINS), 54,* 42–66. http://doi.org/10.17159/2309-8708/2017/n54a4.

Nwoye, A. (2017b). The psychology and content of dreaming in Africa. *Journal of Black Psychology, 43*(1), 3–26. https://doi.org/10.1177/0095798415614159.

Nwoye, A. (2017c). A postcolonial theory of African Psychology: A reply to Kopano Ratele. *Theory & Psychology, 27*(3), 328–36. https://doi.org/10.1177/0959354317700000.

Nwoye, A. (2020). From psychological humanities to African psychology: A review of sources and traditions. In *Oxford research encyclopedia of psychology.* Oxford University Press. https://doi.org/10.1093/acrefore/9780190236557.013.659.

Nwoye, A. (2022). *African psychology: The emergence of a tradition.* Oxford University Press. https://doi.org/10.1093/oso/9780190932497.001.0001.

Opare-Henaku, A., & Utsey, S. O. (2017). Culturally prescribed beliefs about mental illness among the Akan of Ghana. *Transcultural Psychiatry, 54*(4), 502–22. https://doi.org/10.1177/1363461517708120/

Oppong, S. (2011). *Health & safety: Theory and practice in the oil and gas sector.* VDM Verlag Dr Müller.

Oppong, S. (2013a). Industrial and organizational psychology in Ghana. *The Industrial-Organizational Psychologist, 50*(3), 79–83. https://doi.org/10.1037/e520182013-009.

Oppong, S. (2013b). Indigenizing knowledge for development: Epistemological and pedagogical approaches. *Africanus, 4*(2), 34–50. https://doi.org/10.25159/0304-615X/2300.

Oppong, S. (2014). A critique of the philosophical underpinnings of mainstream social science research. *Academicus, 5*(10), 242–54. https://doi.org/10.7336/academicus.2014.10.17.

Oppong, S. (2015a). A critique of early childhood development research and practice in Africa. *Africanus, 45*(1), 23–41. https://doi.org/10.25159/0304-615X/252.

Oppong, S. (2015b). Risk chain process model: Linking risk perception to occupational accidents. *Sigurnost, 57*(1), 25–34. https://hrcak.srce.hr/137603.

Oppong, S. (2016). The journey towards Africanizing psychology in Ghana. *Psychological Thought, 9*(1), 1–14. https://psyct.swu.bg/index.php/psyct/article/view/128/html.

Oppong, S. (2017). History of psychology in Ghana since 989 AD. *Psychological Thought, 10*(1), 7–48. https://psyct.swu.bg/index.php/psyct/article/view/195/html.

Oppong, S. (2018). Investigating comprehension of road hazard communication designs and safety climate as correlates of risk perception and road traffic accidents using mixed methods design. In *Sage research methods cases part 2*. Sage Publications Ltd. https://doi.org/10.4135/9781526439079.

Oppong, S. (2019a). Overcoming obstacles to a truly global psychological theory, research and praxis in Africa. *Journal of Psychology in Africa, 29* (4), 292–300. https://doi.org/10.1080/14330237.2019.1647497.

Oppong, S. (2019b). Doing 'history of psychology' in Ghana: A long, frustrating, lonely journey without directional signs but rewarding. *HAP: Newsletter of History of Applied Psychology, 10*, 4–8. https://iaapsy.org/site/assets/files/1820/newsletter_10_june_2019.pdf.

Oppong, S. (2019c). When the ethical is unethical and the unethical is ethical: Cultural relativism in ethical decision-making. *Polish Psychological Bulletin, 50*(1), 18–28. https://doi.org/10.24425/ppb.2019.126014.

Oppong, S. (2020a). When something dehumanizes, it is violent but when it elevates, it is not violent. *Theory & Psychology, 30*(3), 468–72. https://doi.org/10.1177/0959354320920942.

Oppong, S. (2020b). Towards a model of valued human cognitive abilities: An African perspective based on a systematic review. *Frontiers in Psychology, 11*, 538072. https://doi.org/10.3389/fpsyg.2020.538072.

Oppong, S. (2021a). From risk perception to accident: An empirical test of the risk chain process model. *Sigurnost, 63*(2), 125–42. https://doi.org/10.31306/s.63.2.1.

Oppong, S. (2021b). Development and testing of culturally adapted road hazard communication designs. *International Journal of Occupational Safety and Ergonomics, 27*(1), 290–301. https://doi.org/10.1080/10803548.2019.1573942.

Oppong, S. (2022a). Indigenous psychology in Africa: Centrality of culture, misunderstandings, and global positioning. *Theory & Psychology, 32*(6), 953–73. https://doi.org/10.1177/09593543221097334.

Oppong, S. (2022b). On mainstreaming philosophy of science in psychology through 'psychological theoretics'. *Annals of Psychology, XXV*(1), 27–45. https://doi.org/10.18290/rpsych2022.0002.

Oppong, S. (2022c). Raising a new generation in a postcolonial era through decolonised early childhood development and care services. *Contemporary Issues in Early Childhood, 23*(2), 182–97. https://doi.org/10.1177/1463949120970238.

Oppong, S. (2023a). Epistemological allyship. *Psychology and Developing Societies*, *35*(1), 69–86. https://doi.org/10.1177/09713336231152301.

Oppong, S. (2023b). An indigenous representation of personhood for citizenship behaviours. In J. Osafo & C. S. Akotia (Eds.), *Personhood, Community and the human condition: Reflections and applications in the African experience* (pp. 27–47). Ayebia Clarke Publishing Limited.

Oppong, S. (2023c). Promoting global ECD top-down and bottom-up. *Ethos, 51* (3), 321–5. https://doi.org/10.1111/etho.12393.

Oppong, S., Ajei, M. O., & Majeed, H. M. (2023). Nurturing the nexus between African philosophy and African psychology. *The American Philosophical Association Studies*, *23*(1), 141–6. https://cdn.ymaws.com/www.apaonline .org/resource/collection/C29D5481-4D0D-4E09-81F3-8C5DC2148822/ APAStudiesFall2023.pdf.

Oppong, S., Asante, K. O., & Anum, A. (2022). Psychological assessment in West Africa. In S. Laher (Ed.), *International histories of psychological assessment* (Educational and Psychological Testing in a Global Context, pp. 59–81). Cambridge University Press. https://doi.org/10.1017/9781108755078.005.

Oppong, S., Brune, K. R., & Mpofu, E. (2020). Indigenous community health. In E. Mpofu (Ed.), *Sustainable community health: Systems and practices in diverse settings* (pp. 579–610). Palgrave Macmillan. https://doi.org/10.1007/ 978-3-030-59687-3_17.

Oppong, S., Oppong Asante, K., & Kumaku, S. K. (2014). History, development and current status of psychology in Ghana. In C. S. Akotia & C.C. Mate-Kole (Eds). *Contemporary psychology: Readings from Ghana* (pp. 1–17). Digibooks Ghana Ltd.

Oppong, S., & Strader, S. (2022). *Interventions that matter start with local cultures: Issues and strategies in early childhood care and education interventions in Africa.* An ECCE Project Supported by Spencer Foundation/ Boston College. https://doi.org/10.13140/RG.2.2.12651.82722/1.

Oppong Asante, K., & Oppong, S. (2012). Psychology in Ghana. *Journal of Psychology in Africa*, *22*(3), 473–8. https://doi.org/10.1080/14330237.2012 .10820557.

Osei-Tutu, A., Dzokoto, V. A., Adams, G., et al. (2018). 'My own house, car, my husband, and children': Meanings of success among Ghanaians. *Heliyon, 4* (7), e00696. https://doi.org/10.1016/j.heliyon.2018.e00696.

Osei-Tutu, A., Dzokoto, V. A., Affram, A. A., et al. (2020). Cultural models of well-being implicit in four Ghanaian languages. *Frontiers in Psychology, 11*, 1798. https://doi.org/10.3389/fpsyg.2020.01798.

Owusu, M. K. (2012). Towards an African critique of African ethnography: The usefulness of the useless. In H. Lauer & K. Anyidoho (Eds.), *Reclaiming the human sciences and humanities through African perspectives* (pp. 77–104). Sub-Saharan Publishers.

Pasricha, S. K. (2011). Relevance of para-psychology in psychiatric practice. *Indian Journal of Psychiatry, 53*(1), 4–8. https://doi.org/10.4103/0019-5545 .75544.

Pence, A., Makokoro, P., Ebrahim, H. B., & Barry, O. (Eds.). (2023). *Sankofa: Appreciating the past in planning the future of early childhood education, care and development in Africa.* United Nations Educational, Scientific and Cultural Organization. https://unesdoc.unesco.org/ark:/48223/ pf0000384942.

Pheko, M., Oppong, S., & Mfolwe, L. (2021). Substance use in organizations: Antecedents and interventions. In M. M. Mutepfa (Ed.), S*ubstance use and misuse in sub-Saharan Africa: Trends, intervention, and policy* (pp. 113–28). Palgrave Macmillan. https://doi.org/10.1007/978-3-030-85732-5_8.

Phuti, F., Tsheko, G. N., & Oppong, S. (2023). Developing and validating a soft skills assessment scale for psychoeducational assessment. *Sage Open, 13*(4), 1–15.

Pickren, W. E., & Taşçı, G. (2022). Indigenous psychologies: Resources for future histories. In D. McCallum (Ed.), *The Palgrave handbook of the history of human sciences* (pp. 1–22). Palgrave Macmillan. https://doi.org/10.1007/ 978-981-15-4106-3_80-2.

Poortinga, Y. H. (2021). *Concept and method in cross-cultural and cultural psychology.* Cambridge University Press. https://doi.org/10.1017/97811 08908320.

Rad, M. S., Martingano, A. J., & Ginges, J. (2018). Toward a psychology of Homo sapiens: Making psychological science more representative of the human population. *Proceedings of the National Academy of Sciences of the United States of America, 115*(45), 11401–11405. https://doi.org/10.1073/ pnas.1721165115.

Ratele, K. (2017a). Editorial: Frequently asked questions about African psychology. *South African Journal of Psychology, 47*(3), 273–9. https://doi .org/10.1177/0081246317703249.

Ratele, K. (2017b). Editorial: Six theses on African psychology for the world. *Psychology in Society, 54,* 1–9. www.scielo.org.za/scielo.php?script= sci_arttext&pid=S1015-60462017000200001.

Ratele, K. (2017c). Four (African) psychologies. *Theory & Psychology, 27*(3), 313–27. https://doi.org/10.1177/0959354316684215.

Roughley, N. (2021). Human nature. In E. N. Zalta (Ed.), *The Stanford encyclopedia of philosophy* (Spring 2021 Edition). https://plato.stanford.edu/arch ives/spr2021/entries/human-nature/.

Russell, R., Chung, M., Balk, E. M., et al. (2009). *Issues and challenges in conducting systematic reviews to support development of nutrient reference values: Workshop summary.* (Prepared by the Tufts Evidence-based Practice Center under Contract No.290–02-0022).

AHRQ Publication No. 09–0026-2. Agency for Healthcare Research and Quality.

Sam, D. L. (2014). Relationship between culture and behaviour. In C. S. Akotia & C. C. Mate-Kole (Eds.), *Contemporary psychology: Readings from Ghana* (pp. 231–47). Digibooks Ghana.

Samuelson, B. L. (2009). Ventriloquation in discussions of student writing: Examples from a high school English class. *Research in the Teaching of English, 44*(1), 52–88. www.jstor.org/stable/27784349.

Scheidecker, G., Boyette, A., Chaudhary, N., et al. (2023b). Parents, caregivers, and peers: Patterns of complementarity in the social world of children in rural Madagascar (article, comments, and reply). *Current Anthropology, 64*(3). www.journals.uchicago.edu/doi/10.1086/725037.

Scheidecker, G., Chaudhary, N., Keller, H., et al. (2023). Poor brain development' in the Global South? Challenging the science of early childhood interventions. *Ethos: Journal of the Society for Psychological Anthropology, 51*(1), 1–24. https://doi.org/10.1111/etho.12379.

Scheidecker, G., Chaudhary, N., Oppong, S., et al. (2022). Different is not deficient: Respecting diversity in early childhood development. *The Lancet: Child & Adolescent Health, 6*(12), e24–e25. https://doi.org/10.1016/S2352-4642(22)00277-2.

Scheidecker, G., Oppong, S., Chaudhary, N., & Keller, H. (2021). How overstated scientific claims undermine ethical principles in parenting interventions. *BMJ Global Health, 6*(9). http://doi.org/10.1136/bmjgh-2021-007323.

Scheidecker, G., Tekola, B., Rasheed, M., et al. (2024). Ending epistemic exclusion: Toward a truly global science and practice of early childhood development. *The Lancet: Child & Adolescent Health, 8*(1), 3–5. https://doi.org/10.1016/S2352-4642(23)00292-4.

Schein, E. H. (1984, January 15). Coming to a new awareness of organizational culture. *Sloan Management Review, 25*(2), 3–16. https://sloanreview.mit.edu/article/coming-to-anew-awareness-of-organizational-culture/.

Schein, E. H. (2004). *Organizational culture and leadership* (3rd ed.). John Wiley & Sons.

Schultz, D. P., & Schultz, S. E. (2012). *A history of modern psychology* (10th ed.). Wadsworth.

Serpell, R. (1989). 'Dimensions endogenes de l'intelligence chez les AChewa et autres peuples Africains [Endogenous dimensions of intelligence among

AChewa and other African peoples]. In J. Retschitzki, M. B. Lagos, & P. Dasen (Eds.), *La Recherche Interculturelle, Tome II* [Intercultural Research, Vol. II] (pp. 164–79). Editions l'Harmattan.

Serpell, R. (1993). *The significance of schooling: Life-journeys in an African society.* Cambridge University Press.

Serpell, Z. N., Dzokoto, V. A. A, Anum, A., & Belgrave, F. Z. (2022). Editorial: African cultural models in psychology. *Frontiers in Psychology, 13*, 844872. https://doi.org/10.3389/fpsyg.2022.844872.

Shadish, W. R., Cook, T. D., & Campbell, D. T. (2002). *Experimental and quasi experimental designs for generalized causal inference.* Houghton Mifflin Company.

Simpson, M. C., Majeed, H. M., Ackah, K., & E. I. Ani E. I. (Eds.). (2013). *A celebration of philosophy & classics.* Ayebia Clarke Publishing.

Singh, L., Cristia, A., Karasik, L. B., et al. (2023). Diversity and representation in infant research: Barriers and bridges toward a globalized science of infant development. *Infancy: The Official Journal of the International Society on Infant Studies, 28*(4), 708–37. https://doi.org/10.1111/infa.12545.

Smith, J. A. (2015). *Qualitative psychology: A practical guide to research methods* (3rd ed.). Sage.

Spencer-Oatey, H. (2008). *Culturally speaking: Culture, communication and politeness theory* (2nd ed.). Continuum.

Ssentongo, J. S. (2020). 'Which journal is that?' Politics of academic promotion in Uganda and the predicament of African publication outlets. *Critical African Studies, 12*(3), 283–301. https://doi.org/10.1080/21681392.2020.1788400.

Starodub, A. (2015). Post-representational epistemology in practice: Processes of relational knowledge creation in autonomous social movements. *Interface: A Journal for and about Social Movements, 7*(2), 161–91. www.interfacejournal.net/wordpress/wp-content/uploads/2015/12/Issue-7-2-Starodub.pdf.

Steindl, C., Jonas, E., Sittenthaler, S., et al. (2015). Understanding psychological reactance: New developments and findings. *Zeitschrift fur Psychologie, 223*(4), 205–14. https://doi.org/10.1027/2151-2604/a000222.

Tafirenyika, J., Mhizha, S., & Ejuu, G. (2023). Building inclusive early learning environments for children with a disability in low-resource settings: Insights into challenges and opportunities from rural Zimbabwe. *Frontiers in Education, 8*, 1029076. https://doi.org/10.3389/feduc.2023.1029076.

Taylor, C. (1992). *Sources of the self: The making of the modern identity.* Cambridge University Press.

Teo, T., & Febbraro, A. R. (2003). Ethnocentrism as a form of intuition in psychology. *Theory & Psychology, 13*(5), 673–94. https://doi.org/10.1177/09593543030135009.

Thalmayer, A. G., Toscanelli, C., & Arnett, J. J. (2021). The neglected 95% revisited: Is American psychology becoming less American? *American Psychologist*, *76*(1), 116–29. https://doi.org/10.1037/amp0000622.

Tsamaase, M., Harkness, S., & Super, C. M. (2020). Grandmothers' developmental expectations for early childhood in Botswana. *New Directions for Child and Adolescent Development*, *2020*(170), 93–112. https://doi.org/10.1002/cad.20335.

UNICEF. (2021). *Baseline study for the community-based integrated early childhood development (ECD) 'Insaka' programme.* www.unicef.org/zam bia/reports/baseline-study-community-based-integrated-early-childhood-development-insaka-programme.

United Nations. (2004, January). *The concept of Indigenous peoples.* Background paper prepared by the Secretariat of the Permanent Forum on Indigenous Issues. www.un.org/esa/socdev/unpfii/documents/workshop_da ta_background.doc

Weber, A. M., Diop, Y., Gillespie, D., et al. (2021). Africa is not a museum: The ethics of encouraging new parenting practices in rural communities in low-income and middle-income countries. *BMJ Global Health*, *6*(7), e006218. https://doi.org/10.1136/bmjgh-2021-006218.

Whorf, B. L. (1956). Science and linguistics. In J. B. Carroll (Ed.), *Language, thought, and reality* (pp. 207–19). MIT Press.

Wingo, A. (2017). Akan philosophy of the person. In Edward N. Zalta (Ed.), *The Stanford encyclopedia of philosophy* (Summer 2017 Edition). https://plato.stanford.edu/archives/sum2017/entries/akan-person/.

Wiredu, K. (Ed.). (2004). *A companion to African philosophy.* Blackwell Publishing.

Wiredu, K. (2013). Are there cultural universals? In M. C. Simpson, H. M. Majeed, K. Ackah, & E. I. Ani (Eds.), *A Celebration of Philosophy & Classics* (pp. 97–112). Ayebia Clarke Publishing.

Wissing, M. P., Wilson Fadiji, A., Schutte, L., et al. (2020). Motivations for relationships as sources of meaning: Ghanaian and South African experiences. *Frontiers in Psychology, 11*. https://doi.org/10.3389/fpsyg.2020 .02019.

Yang, K.-S. (2012). Indigenous psychology, Westernized psychology, and indigenized psychology: A non-Western psychologist's view. *Chang Gung Journal of Humanities and Social Sciences*, *5*(1), 1–32. https://cgjhsc.cgu .edu.tw/data_files/5-1%2001.pdf.

Yankah, K. (2012). Globalisation and the African scholar. In H. Lauer & K. Anyidoho (Eds.), *Reclaiming the human sciences and humanities through African perspectives* (pp. 51–64). Sub-Saharan Publishers.

Cambridge Elements ≡

Psychology and Culture

Kenneth D. Keith

University of San Diego

Kenneth D. Keith is author or editor of more than 160 publications on cross-cultural psychology, quality of life, intellectual disability, and the teaching of psychology. He was the 2017 president of the Society for the Teaching of Psychology.

About the Series

Elements in Psychology and Culture features authoritative surveys and updates on key topics in cultural, cross-cultural, and indigenous psychology. Authors are internationally recognized scholars whose work is at the forefront of their subdisciplines within the realm of psychology and culture.

Cambridge Elements ☰

Psychology and Culture

Elements in the Series

A full series listing is available at: www.cambridge.org/EPAC

Printed in the United States
by Baker & Taylor Publisher Services